Conflict Recovery

Conflict Recovery

Cultural Humility and Civility in Education

Dr. Candice Dowd Barnes,
Chayla Rutledge Slaton,
and Todd Scott Parker

ROWMAN & LITTLEFIELD
Lanham • Boulder • New York • London

Published by Rowman & Littlefield
An imprint of The Rowman & Littlefield Publishing Group, Inc.
4501 Forbes Boulevard, Suite 200, Lanham, Maryland 20706
www.rowman.com

6 Tinworth Street, London SE11 5AL, United Kingdom

Copyright © 2020 by Candice Dowd Barnes, Chayla Rutledge, and Todd Scott Parker

All rights reserved. No part of this book may be reproduced in any form or by any electronic or mechanical means, including information storage and retrieval systems, without written permission from the publisher, except by a reviewer who may quote passages in a review.

British Library Cataloguing in Publication Information Available

Library of Congress Cataloging-in-Publication Data Available

ISBN 978-1-4758-5436-7 (cloth : alk. paper)
ISBN 978-1-4758-5437-4 (pbk. : alk. paper)
ISBN 978-1-4758-5438-1 (electronic)

Contents

Preface	vii
Acknowledgments	xi
SECTION I: WHY THIS TOPIC?	**1**
1 A Context of the Issue	3
2 The Demographic Shift Reframing Diversity, Equity, and Inclusion	13
3 Understanding Cultural Humility and Civility	21
4 The Need for Cultural Humility and Civility in Education	31
5 Making the Change	43
SECTION II: FOR THE CULTURE: IMPLEMENTING CONFLICT RECOVERY IN SCHOOLS	**53**
6 Teaching: Cultural Humility and Civility in the Classroom	55
7 Leading: Understanding the Cultural SHIFTS	71
8 Counseling: Cultural Humility for the Mental Health Professional in Schools	85
9 Considerations for Higher Education	99
10 Bringing It All Together	107
About the Authors	113

Preface

This book was written with one overall goal in mind: influencing the reader to seek substantive ways to disrupt, or at the very least interrupt, the structural and systemic challenges schools face to engage equity and inclusion regularly. This book is certainly not the only answer. It does however offer the notion that when one practices cultural humility and civility in ways that value and respect humanity, one might be closer to witnessing equity, even if the positive change affects a small population of people.

Change can be difficult but necessary. It is the authors' hope that as the reader engages with each chapter, he or she will make substantive connections to inform decisions and practices about how conflict is managed and humility is central to the school's culture. Schools are one of the oldest systems in the country. Schools are also a system that has operated the same for centuries and were designed to educate based upon the social and economic constructs within a community. However, as society changes, new technologies developed, and the needs of students evolve, so too should schools.

It is an expectation that schools are preparing students to enter the world ready to be social change agents, productive citizens, and enlightened individuals. It is an expectation that schools are developing its members—students and staff—to affect their local and global communities in an effective way. When the members of the school's culture are experiencing cultural conflicts, with limited opportunities for understanding and recovery, the promotion of social change can be a difficult task.

Just connecting the word conflict with recovery can cause dissonance because it can be difficult for people to recover when they have experienced a hurt, a trauma, or a disrespectful comment, for example. We suggest that it is possible. We also suggest that balancing conflict with compromise might be the best one can achieve. However, when practicing cultural humility one can more easily find themselves moving away from a collision. It might be that they never reach a collision because they understand who they are and who the other person is without other-izing them and holding them to generalizations and stereotypes.

In this book, the authors will attempt to make a case for schools to implement practices and principles that will guide high-engagement relationships through cultural humility and civility. The reader will explore the origins of cultural humility, the intersection of cultural humility and civility, and how the concept is applicable to education. Schools are changing. The tides of change should be allowed to wash onto shore and bring back to sea waves of what we want schools to be, how we want school to operate, and educate students to be exactly who they can be and to do so with support from educators who cultivate their potential.

Throughout the book, you will engage in the life of Brookdale High—a fictitious school with real problems and solutions reflected in schools across the country. You will experience the struggles of teachers, students, leaders, and counselors as they attempt to find a way to build a culture—an ethos, that supports its members through various thinking, behaviors, and actions all designed to achieve one desired goal: equity, inclusion, and success for all.

After reading this book, the authors hope that you will:

- Understand how cultural humility and civility are essential in today's educational institutions—K–12 through higher education.
- Identify the intersection of cultural humility and civility.
- Acknowledge issues and potential, and criticize the educational system to ensure equity and inclusion are realized.
- Recognize the role that each person—students, staff, parents, other professionals, and support staff—has in creating a thriving ethos and culture.
- Examine one's own bias and potential cultural conflicts.
- Continually engage in cultural humility and make it a core practice.

- Make connections with the concepts presented to strengthen one's knowledge and skills in conflict recovery.
- Share the information with other school personnel to develop practices and procedures that reflect conflict recovery and restoration in the school setting.
- Replace language and schemes of thinking about people designed to otherize them.
- Promote intentional and purposeful civility—thinking, action, and behavior—that respects and values humanity.
- Think, reflect, and connect often with the concepts presented to evaluate one's own practices.
- Use the activities presented in the book to engage conversation and dialogue about restorative practices and conflict recovery.
- Recognize the benefit of high-engagement relationships.
- Promote the idea of conflict recovery within your circle of educators, friends, and colleagues to make recovery a normalized part of any school's culture

Acknowledgments

This book is a literary commitment to our collective desire to be a change enterprise—a person or a group of people engaged in intentional and purposeful actions to shift thinking, behaviors, and actions toward a greater good. There are countless conversations, discussions, and thinking that brought this book together and although we cannot name every single person, we hope you all know how truly grateful we are to you all. We do want to thank a few people who have been, and continue to be, our constant cheerleaders and coaches throughout this process.

From Chayla: I would like to thank my husband, Ray Slaton. You have spent countless hours editing my work and offering words of encouragement and support when it felt like nothing was going right. You have been a rock through everything and have selflessly offered up your time and energy to be my teammate. I would also like to thank my parents, Brent and Joy Rutledge, for raising me to see everyone as a unique individual, despite skin color, ability status, SES, and so on, and for teaching me to always advocate for what is right.

Finally, I would like to thank my mentors, Dr. Candice Barnes and Dr. Patty Kohler-Evans, for giving me opportunities and for helping me find my voice, and for your guidance and continual support beyond the necessary scope of your jobs.

From Candice: I am forever grateful to a powerful and courageous mother. You are my greatest champion and ally. Thank you to my family and friends who keep me honest and always questioning what more can I do to be in service to others. Thank you to my coauthors. You all have been true collaborators on this, and many other topics. We will get started on the next projects tomorrow! And thank you, Love, for wearing the cape whenever I need a superhero.

From Todd: I'd like to thank my dad, James Parker, for his gene of patient tenacity. I'm not sure if he actually coined the term "stick-to-it-tiveness," but over time, and through osmosis, I've prospered from his modeling. A true champion in the dad department. Ms. Shelly Pelts, you were a crucial participant in my conflict recovery experience, and a living example of the proven strategies found in this book.

We also want to dedicate this to all of those who join us in disrupting and interrupting systems of inequity and oppression. We profess that education should never be one of those systems. Sadly, it is. However, we can make the choice to change it or maintain the status quo. So, to educators working with young people every day to help them find their pathways toward success, this book is for you!

Section I

WHY THIS TOPIC?

The need for humility, equity, and inclusion is at a premium in today's schools. This book will present a case for grounding a school's culture in these concepts through cultural humility, civility, and conflict recovery. This first section is comprised of five chapters. Each chapter not only scaffolds and builds a case for cultural humility and civility in education but also provides strategies, activities, and concepts to change the language used to guide positive behavioral supports and opportunities for restorative justice.

The introduction provides a general overview of the book and presents some of the key terms and ideas that will be discussed throughout. Following the introduction is a thorough discussion of cultural humility and civility. The subsequent chapters make a case for including both concepts, cultural humility and civility, in educational settings. The goal is to increase the reader's understanding—his or her awareness of cultural humility. In particular, these chapters attempt to address why conflict recovery can help support the teaching, leading, and counseling aspects in schools.

At the end of each chapter, the authors provide a section with reflection questions, and for some chapters, there are activities to help the reader utilize the concepts effectively. Most importantly, as the reader moves into section II, these foundational chapters will allow for a deeper dive into realizing the benefit of humility, equity, and inclusion in K–12 education and in higher education.

Chapter 1

A Context of the Issue

The man who knows something, know he knows nothing at all.

Erykah Badu

This chapter will help the reader:

- Understand why this topic is important across educational settings.
- Explore the shift from diversity, equity, and inclusion to a more in-depth focus on humility.
- Recognize a context of the issues driving the need for more humility and opportunities for empathy and understanding to promote positive interactions and relationships.
- Implement strategies and activities to enhance his or her practices, and the policies within the school. More insights will be offered later in this chapter.

This chapter generally underwrites the need for educators to effectively respond to the shifting demographics especially in K–12 schools that will change the social and cultural landscape of this country. While chapter 2 presents a detailed discussion of the demographic shifts in education, this chapter lays the foundation for educators to begin thinking about how they view their own beliefs and values and those of others.

By discussing the issues and challenges that support implementing cultural humility and civility, educators can embark upon intentional and purposeful actions that have the potential to affect the trajectory of relationships and academic success of students. Using these ideas as the foundations on which schools achieve recovery and restoration is essential to the overall shift to ensure a deeper understanding of self and others.

Still, you may be asking, "How will this information influence my practices, knowledge and skills?" This book is written to offer strategies, information, and ideas to help with the following:

- Enter and exit conversations about challenging topics, especially conversations that address race and culture.
- Understand how to engage in cultural humility that affects thinking, behavior, and actions.
- Implement strategies and activities to address stereotypes, biases, and misinterpretations about identity types.
- Explore strategies to engage restorative justice practices and recovery in the classroom and school.
- Manage the culture and climate by attending to the SHIFTS in the ethos.

GLOSSARY OF TERMS

Throughout the book, the authors will introduce some commonly used terms. However, the authors offer different perspectives, approaches, or a slightly different way of thinking about the terms. Each term will be explained in the future chapters. Brief explanations of the terms are given below.

Bias Boundaries—the values and beliefs which guide one's interactions, relationships, and practices. The term addresses the way in which values, beliefs, and ethos support or challenge biases. It also addresses the need for belonging and social group norms.
Civility—thinking, action, and behavior that respects and values humanity.
Conflict—a quarrel or disagreement meant to be resolved for growth and progress to occur.
Conflict Recovery—a process of mindfulness and behavioral changes to avoid apathy, assumptions, arrogance, and the acidic commentary that only drives individuals further apart. The process that moves along a continuum from reflection to rebuilding.

Culturalism—an ideology that describes an individual who is shaped by their culture and whose behavior reflects that of their culture.

Cultural Humility—an approach that fosters self-renewal and reflection and an authentic undertaking to understand the lives of others to develop authentic relationships, interactions, and to serve individuals effectively.

Ethos—the way in which the cultural spirit is manifested through values and beliefs of the people who are the members of the culture.

Humility—freedom from arrogance, assumptions, and acidic commentary. It is attribute that fosters vulnerability and flexibility.

Other-izing—applying stereotypes, biases, generalizations, and other methods to categorize people and label them.

High-engagement relationship—flexible, resilient, and authentic relatedness central to recovery. The relationship is based on an openness to practice cultural humility daily.

Recovery and Restoration—offering the opportunity to return to a desired state or find a new path toward positive or desired behavior.

Identity Protectionism—based on the concept of identity protective cognition. Identity protectionism is a retreating to comfortable spaces and known narratives when one feels threatened.

These terms and concepts will be discussed and described in detail. The authors provide this new way of thinking with the hope that the reader will internalize a new meaning and a new way of thinking about conflict, recovery, humility, and civility. Ultimately, the goal is for the reader to see each term as action-oriented and solution-focused. Let us continue building a context with a discussion about conflict.

CONFLICT AT ITS CORE

Conflict is a disagreement or quarrel. However, too often, conflict quickly turns into confrontations, and sometimes, collisions when it goes unchecked. When the conflict reaches a state of collision, it typically happens because people have no understanding of the person or persons with whom they have the conflict. They may not understand the person's background, history, or circumstances. This may cause a breakdown of communication or can negatively affect opportunities for civility, humility, or empathy, and the ability to offer recovery and restoration to one another.

In addition, there may not be an understanding of the person's discussion style or conflict style. Discussion and conflict style have cultural and behavioral attributes that might explain the gestures, antics, body language, tone, and movements—all that reflects the way in which an individual engages in a conversation or discussion and when that individual might be in conflict with his or her conversation partner.

This may expedite a person's retreating from opportunities where *recovery—returning to a desired state of being*—can be beneficial to both parties. If the retreat occurs, the road back to a healthy relationship is long and littered with assumptions about one's behavior, which could move the conflict to a confrontation or collision. When a collision happens, especially a cultural collision, it can be almost impossible to find easy and quick pathways toward recovery.

There are many reasons why conflicts occur. Most conflicts happen, however, because of a lack of understanding or compromise. It might also happen because individuals make assumptions about someone else with limited evidence about who the person is beyond their identities (i.e., race, ethnicity, orientation, disability, and so on), or their perceived way of behaving. These assumptions are typically based on superficial attributes, stereotypes, and previous experiences or encounters with a single person. That single experience is normalized for an entire group of people. This is dangerous, unfortunate, and robs people of the richness one gains when they get to know other people.

This can be especially true when one relies on past experiences with other people or media portrayals of groups of people, especially if those persons share the same or similar identities with each other. For example, if you have a negative experience with, or have seen, African American males portrayed as criminals, you may generalize some of those negative thoughts to most African American men you encounter.

When someone relies solely on their limited experiences, that can be an acute problem in schools, where people from diverse backgrounds and experiences interact daily. It is further compounded when dealing with students and teachers who encounter systematic, implicit, and daily traumas.

Imagine what may occur in a classroom of predominantly African American male students and a teacher who has limited exposure to African

American men except for one uncomfortable experience and constant images of African American men in the media as dangerous, criminal, aggressive, and threatening. Imagine what happens to people's thinking and emotions when those images and understandings are perpetuated throughout history.

Here is another example. Imagine you have interacted with a person with a physical disability. That interaction resulted in their needing your assistance. That singular and limited experience could potentially shape your thinking about all people with a physical disability needing help. Certainly, this is untrue and can be offensive or at the very least, negatively affect the person with the disability. It might also change the nature of your relationship with them.

A final example for cultural context. Assume that the scope of your understanding about farmworkers is that those individuals are undocumented criminals. That stereotype could shape your future interactions and understandings about a group of people. It might even arrest your ability to see a person's humanity beyond a label or stereotype.

This type of phenomenon is increasingly present in schools. Why? Schools are a microcosm of our society and the world in which we live. Students and staff from diverse backgrounds, histories, and identities commune in the same place for nine months. In many ways, schools reflect the "melting pot" of America and still may be quite segregated, especially when it comes to race and culture. A recent documentary, *America to Me*, explored and examined the social and racial equity issues students experienced that reflected their larger community and societal challenges.

For this chapter, and the book overall, the authors will begin to make a case for activities, strategies, and approaches to increase cultural humility and civility in education that will guide how people engage in conflict recovery. The authors will explain the challenges of conforming to one's bias boundaries and retreating to identity protectionism. There will also be an exploration of the propensity for individuals to come into agreement when simply understanding is the desired goal. This propensity for agreement can arrest one's ability to realize the elements of cultural humility—awareness, sensitivity, and responsiveness. These elements of cultural humility are discussed in detail in chapter 2.

While this book is not necessarily about racial inequity in education, it is unavoidable, and frankly, a necessary part of the book's discussion. It would be an incomplete essay of thought if not included in the discussion. Race is undoubtedly an uncomfortable topic, but race will frame the context for the book. It is simply a disservice to the reader to attempt to address cultural humility and civility and exclude the complexities of race.

Additionally, the behaviors that will be discussed next—protectionism, bias boundaries, and a desire for agreement can be particularly dangerous when attempting to resolve conflicts predicated on racial, ethnic, and cultural differences. Those concepts are discussed in the next section to continue to build a case for the topic of conflict recovery and using cultural humility and civility to help strategize how best to implement this overall approach in schools.

BIAS BOUNDARIES

Bias boundaries refer to the values, beliefs, and ethos that one conforms to which creates a baseline understanding of self and others. Bias boundaries can be dynamic depending upon the experiences that one has. The boundaries can expand or solidify based on new knowledge and experiences. Moreover, bias boundaries can negatively or positively affect the interactions and relationships one builds and cultivates throughout life.

As one experiences new people, places, and ideologies, their boundaries expand to integrate new concepts and information into one's current scheme of thinking. These boundaries could also lead to the rejection of new ideas if one's values is steadfast and unshakable. In educational settings, these boundaries can expand quickly, which may create cognitive dissonance. It might even cause reluctance to engage in discourse, especially when the information is related to race, equity, and inclusion. This internal struggle to understand self and others may drive emotionality and interactions. It may solidify or stretch these binding boundaries.

For example, imagine that you have been taught to avoid interacting with a certain group of people. Perhaps you were told they were dangerous. Perhaps you have even seen images through various media sources that support what you have been taught. Congenitally, all of your lived and loved experiences happened in a vacuum, and your understanding of this group of people is very narrow.

Then, your family moves to a different community or neighborhood. You are now attending a new high school where the members of that high school are from diverse backgrounds. In your chemistry class, your teacher partners you with someone from the "other" group for a project. This person whom you've always seen as "other," is the exact opposite of everything you were taught and observed through media. How do you address the confusion—the cognitive and emotional dissonance you might be feeling? This is the challenge of seeing others through your narrow view without giving someone else the opportunity to express their narrative, history, and experience.

The authors suggest that instead of these narrow views, what *should* be considered is elevated through cultural humility and civility, first. It is authentic, and perhaps, an intentional discovery of self and others that renews with each new experience and new insights that are specific to an individual. In other words, no two people are alike, not even twins. Recognizing the authenticity and organic way in which cultural humility affords one the opportunity to build relationships beyond the bias boundaries is paramount.

The authors submit that bias boundaries are essential to understanding the traditional ways in which one shapes their identities and personalities and acknowledges the identities of others. Another nuance of bias boundaries is those values and beliefs one holds might be used to generalize a person or a group of people. It may also be that those boundaries are based on the limitations of one's experiences with other people. However, those boundaries are fluid and flexible and should allow for new thoughts, ideas, and understandings to continue to shape one's knowledge and experiences.

Bias Boundaries, Protectionism, and Conflict

Conflicts can occur when one retreats to their bias boundaries. It can also happen when one has not embraced the concept of continued self-discovery, which, as will be discussed in chapter 2, is key to cultural humility. Moreover, when one does not engage in offering others grace and recovery, the conflict can further erect barriers between individuals and can continue to erode the potential for healthy relationships to evolve. Unfortunately, when one adds racial inequity to the mix, the conflict and pathways toward recovery can become even more complex and uncomfortable.

In school settings, conflicts occur daily, hourly, and there can be multiple conflicts happening simultaneously between teachers, students, parents, and other professionals. Any human being who is a part of the school's culture and climate may have a conflict with someone, especially when these individuals are forced to work in challenging or toxic environments built on unhealthy and disingenuous relationships. And because schools can be very diverse, those various identities, binaries, and chosen affinity groups can become a major factor in how people understand, interact with, and think about, one another.

This is a major source of misunderstanding and disagreement, particularly when people do not extend beyond limited interactions with others. When peeling back the layers related to conflict, almost nothing creates more discomfort and visceral feeling than race. Our current state of being in America dangles precariously on the edge of racial tension, cultural biases, and *identity protectionism*—retreating to comfortable and known understandings of others in an attempt to protect one's identity, thinking, and behavior as superior or correct. This term is based on the idea of identity-protective cognition. Identity-protective cognition is a complex concept that addresses the tendency to be loyal to our affinity groups in an attempt to avoid risking influence by other patterns of thinking or behaving (Kahan, 2017).

The authors of this book propose a shift in thinking about how we handle conflict by first engaging in cultural humility and civility to foster high-engagement relationships with others. It is also a fostering of ones attempt to deepen the understanding of self and others. The hope is that such fostering of engagement will allow richer conversations to grow. The hope is also that an individual will work toward action and not just talk about what is wrong. This move toward action is at the core of conflict recovery. It is the strong desire to find a space where one engages in resolve.

Additionally, diversity science researchers theorize increased fertility and migration trends, coupled with the "majority-minority crossover" (p. 78), as cited in (Plaut, 2010), and the shifts occurring in the American workforce, create tensions that may unearth repressed long-held ideologies. Increased access to one another can create further problematic interactions that widen the divide between and among individuals, especially when one's perceived power and livelihoods appears threatened.

Thus, cultural humility can be an incredibly useful and valuable tool for exploration and discovery of self and others. As you explore the next chapter, you will read about the changing demographics and a different view of diversity, equity, and inclusion that reflects the call for diversity science as a way to understand the systemic and structural issues affecting education. However, before you leave this introductory section, examine your own understanding by responding to the think, reflect, and connect questions.

The think, reflect, connect section will be found at the end of each chapter to help promote a shift in thinking, actions, and behaviors. There will be space for you to write down your thoughts so that you can refer back to your thoughts, reflect more deeply, and share your perspectives with your colleagues and others.

THINK, REFLECT, CONNECT

1) How does this information resonate with you thus far, and how might you use these terms to offer different language or a different way to think about conflict to those in your work or school setting?
2) How would you explain the importance of conflict recovery and cultural humility in your school?

_____
_____
_____
_____
_____

REFERENCES

Kahan, D. (2017). Misconceptions, misinformation, and the logic of identity-protective cognition. *Yale Law School. Public Law Research Paper*, 164.

Plaut, V. C. (2010). Diversity science: Why and how difference makes a difference. *Psychological Inquiry, 21*, 77–99. doi: 10.1080/10478401003676501

Chapter 2

The Demographic Shift Reframing Diversity, Equity, and Inclusion

> *"An individual has not started living until he can rise above the narrow confines of his individualistic concerns to the broader concerns of all humanity."*
>
> —*Martin Luther King, Jr.*

The demographic shifts in education will dramatically change over the next few years. In K–12 education, current reports indicate the majority of children under eighteen are students of color. In fact, the National Center for Education Statistics (NCES) predicts that in the year 2024, the racial makeup of public schools will be 46 percent white (down from 51% in 2012), 29 percent Hispanic (up from 24% in 2012), 6 percent Asian/ Pacific Islander (5 % in 2012), and 15 percent black (16% in 2012).

The racial makeup of elementary and secondary teachers, however, is not as diverse as the student population now. That trend will likely continue. In 2012, 82 percent of public school teachers were white, 7 percent were black, and 8 percent were Hispanic. Incidentally, the number of black male teachers is 1 percent of all teachers across the country. This latter statistic is particularly troubling for many reasons, including the fact that there is an overrepresentation of black and brown boys in special education for emotional and behavioral issues. Oftentimes it is a misunderstanding or misinterpretation of discussion and conflict style and the cultural expressiveness that might be viewed as threatening. Again, this is why cultural humility is so vitally important.

What is also troubling is the same differentials with administrators, as reported by NCES. In 2012, 80 percent of public school principals were white, 10 percent were black, and 7 percent were Hispanic. These statistics are important because when addressing educational equity across racial lines, students of color are at a greater disadvantage than their white counterparts. They are oftentimes in schools in economically depressed communities. These students are forced to learn in under-resourced and underfunded schools with limited opportunities and exposure to the best curriculum. They are also, unfortunately, subjected to ideologies and biases that tags their abilities as lesser or inferior to their white peers. Among these startling demographics, the two groups who often find themselves having the greatest challenge are white female teachers and brown, black, and tan young men and boys.

There is a belief among some that the American educational system is built on a level playing field where everyone is free to compete equally. The National Education Association Report (2004) noted three things regarding those assumptions. These assumptions, arguably, may continue to shift the way educators think about how to best educate students, especially those from diverse backgrounds. The assumptions were as follows:

1) Students of color do better academically when taught by teachers of their same ethnicity. Some literature proposes that *all* students, regardless of the students' color, benefit from being taught by teachers of color.
2) Culturally responsive teaching techniques improve academic achievement.
3) Teachers of color have higher achievement expectations for students of color.

The last twenty-five years have seen a shift in education, which has led to the exploration of diversity issues in schools. Color blindness and lack of awareness have led to white educators avoiding the topic of race and the implications for education. This would include not seeing racial issues, not discussing racial issues, and a lack of examining their attitudes toward those who are from different racial and cultural backgrounds. Therefore, if we cannot increase the number of minority teachers we place in the field—in school, we need to prepare white teachers, especially, but also all school professionals from the majority culture to work with students from dissimilar backgrounds.

As schools are increasing in diversity, some individuals are simultaneously avoiding diversity. Others assume that those who are working in diverse educational settings must be culturally competent and comfortable discussing diversity simply because they work in a highly diverse school, have friends of various ethnic and racial makeup, or have attended a diversity training. That is simply untrue. This type of thinking is a disservice to the school system as a whole and further validates the need to embrace cultural humility and civility, and detoxify our understanding of diversity.

DETOXIFYING NARROW VIEWS OF DIVERSITY

Diversity is an evolving field of study. Plaut, (2010), introduces the idea that the deep concerns for the structural racism and disparities are so persistent that realizing the need to engage in *diversity science* may help stem the tide of inequity trends for underrepresented and unrepresented groups of people. According to Plaut, diversity science "should be guided by a sociocultural framework that takes account of cultural and structural realities. . . . A sociocultural paradigm also requires social psychology to address a variety of under examined theoretical assumptions and perspectives. . . . In doing so, diversity science will be able to provide descriptions of diversity-related psychological processes that can help inform practices (p. 78)."

People are generally comfortable with how other people identify themselves and how they connect with certain groups. At least, they pretend to be comfortable with others' self-identification and affiliations. A caveat to this is that the comfortability only extends so far for some. Oftentimes when the bias boundaries are challenged, these same people may retreat to protectionism. Defining diversity as race, culture, ethnicity, gender, orientation, disability, and so on, are all common diversity categories. Those categories of diversity are collectively understood by most people. This is where the greatest comfort lies and where a great deal of diversity training ends for most.

The problem with this idea is the tendency to stay in one's comfort zone and surround themselves with people from similar backgrounds. However, defining diversity is typically where most individuals draw a line and continue to drink from the same well, thus, leaving them intoxicated with the superficial idea of diversity as simply labeling people. This is why the authors suggest that perhaps individuals need to detox their narrow perspectives of diversity to see it as more than labeling.

Furthermore, individuals will withdraw from the need to go deeper and further into issues of equity and inclusion. When pushed to do more than talk about diversity and diversity issues, their action is to create multiple diversity initiatives, projects, and events to celebrate diversity. Yet, the real conversations and work to provide more equity and inclusive practices is overshadowed by the optics of these initiatives, projects, and events. This is counterproductive.

It is akin to diversity window dressing, and frankly, it calls for closing the diversity boutique—a boutique that is quaint, small, and serving only a few clients. Whereas, to continue this analogy, diversity needs to be more like big box stores that are large, vast, numerous, and serving the masses. In fact, engaging in deep discussions about equity, creating substantive practices, policies, and protocols that become normalized, and then celebrating the intensive and extensive ongoing work toward equity and inclusion is more sustainable and meaningful.

EQUITY AND INCLUSION PROHIBITION

America is a highly racialized country. Her citizenry often chose not to engage in learning or acknowledging her painful past. The citizenry often chooses to dismiss or disengage from learning about it's painful past of racial injustice. It is an ugly, hurtful, personal, and shameful truth of our becoming a nation. It is understandable why people would not want to emotionally connect with, experience, or unearth such a painful history. However, it may be necessary to understand the past to move forward toward equity and inclusion.

This has never been a country where "all MEN are created equal." That is simply not true. There were many people left out of that equation. Arguably, American citizens have watched silently as the country fell deeper and deeper into a dark hole of perverse rhetoric and inaction. It has become even more prominently displayed over the last ten years, and certainly, after the election of Barack Obama. Yet, this is changing—a shifting country and America's citizen can do more to interact with dignity and respect.

This systemic, structural horror to oppress people, solely based on skin color, has impacted every institution of our country, especially in education.

In fact, it has only been within the last twenty to thirty years that there has been an exploration of diversity in the educational discipline (Ford & Quinn, 2010). Herein lies the problem with equity and inclusion because equity and inclusion require one to act, not simply talk about that which is already known, like defining diversity.

Fostering equity and inclusion requires work and intentionality. Equity and inclusion afford people the opportunity to maneuver in awkward dialectic spaces where difference of thought and ideas is expressed—spaces that might be challenging and uncomfortable. Simply, equity and inclusion require action, when diversity does not. Diversity only requires one to define the various identities, which categorize people as "the other"—generalizing a person based on personal identities, characteristics, and limitations.

As was mentioned earlier in the chapter, other-izing people only creates more division, puts a fine point on who the person is, and allows for a type of finality predicated on competency. The lack of engaging the concepts of equity and inclusion continues to resuscitate implicit bias, racism, and the marginalization of others by not taking steps to understand one another.

This can be especially dangerous in schools where the concept of equity and inclusion is challenged by cultural and racial anxieties, fixed ideologies about other people, "initiativitis"—saturation and an overabundance of projects and initiatives to no avail, and other issues that preclude people from getting to know each other. Unfortunately, such type of activities is where equity and inclusion go to die.

Equity and inclusion, however, can guide people to move beyond the optics of diversity—compliance, intoxication, and box checking, to actions that demonstrate a cultural shift toward acknowledgment, acceptance, respect, and dignity. Thus, equity and inclusion allow an individual's personal narrative to speak truth and life into dimly lit spaces of indifference, and to do so with confidence. However, it is through the scope of cultural humility, which leads to civility, that equity and inclusion becomes a reality. Still, many overarching questions remain, such as the following:

1) When do we move beyond simply defining over and over again what diversity is, to engaging in how we are going to invest in humanity by practicing humility, equity, and inclusion daily?

2) How do we act upon the patterns of inequity that limit students to find their full potential, teachers to provide a culture for learning in the classroom, administrators to engage in effective and situational leadership that resolves conflict, and counselors to provide wrap-around services for students in crisis?
3) How does engaging these concepts, cultural humility and civility, provide all stakeholders an opportunity for, and tools to implement conflict recovery and restoration?

Answering these questions is no easy task. This is why detoxing your understanding of diversity and building upon the concepts of humility, equity, and inclusion are not boxes that one can check. It requires real action and understanding of others. These concepts affirm or add value to a person's lived and loved experiences. Therefore, to detox the narrow understanding of diversity, in this regard, means to expand the boundaries so that one detours from other-izing people.

Intentional normalization of new schemes of thinking and practicing reflection of how we see each other as people—complex, multilayered, or multi-fractured humans—is crucial to the process. Furthermore, seeing and acknowledging people's obvious and preferred identities with respect undergird the humanity that lives within each and every person. It is through this lens that equity and inclusion are realized and diversity is reframed.

The plain truth is this—equity and inclusion take work! There are no magical strategies, initiatives, or events that can impact the totality of a person's way of being, thinking, and behaving. One has to activate an internal mechanism to seek to understand themselves and others. Moreover, an individual can turn on the homing signal, to guide them toward a different understanding or to deepen the understanding of self. That is certainly a start, but it is a continued journey of renewal, self-awareness, and learning about others in a genuine way.

FINAL THOUGHTS

In closing, by engaging in cultural humility, each person in the learning space can grow, affirm, and share their thoughts and ideas. They can create new knowledge and new perspectives. They can engage in an authentic understanding of others from dissimilar cultural identities, and they can embrace the fluidity of culture and challenge viewpoints that dishonors humanity.

Acknowledging that equity and inclusion require action and a reframing of diversity is a critical step to achieving a deep understanding of self and others. Also, acknowledging and analyzing the systems and structural issues that have historically created schools where inequity thrives and survives must be exercised. It is a thorough examination of diversity as more than a sociocultural construct, but as a science, that has the propensity to challenge thinking and behavior. And it is for all of these reasons why cultural humility and civility can help schools restructure their positive behavior policies or create a healthy culture for learning, living, and creating.

The next chapter will explore and examine the intersection of cultural humility and civility in the larger school context to address the need for conflict recovery, especially to support students' social-emotional development, and citizenship. In the final section of this chapter, the reader is asked to think about, reflect on, and make connections to, the information and their own experiences and develop some next steps.

THINK, REFLECT, CONNECT

1. How would you connect the concepts discussed in this chapter to your own experiences, and how would these concepts have empowered you to understand others?
2. Identity-protective cognition and bias boundaries can negatively affect how we view and interact with one another. What could you do, or have you done, to loosen the binds of those limitations? What could this mean in a highly diverse school with a majority- culture staff?

_____
_____
_____
_____
_____

REFERENCES

Ford, T. N. & Quinn, L. (2010). First-year teachers education candidates: What are their perceptions about multicultural education? *Multicultural Education, 17*(4), 18–24.

Kahan, D. (2017). Misconceptions, misinformation, and the logic of identity-protective cognition. *Yale Law School. Public Law Research Paper*, 164.

Plaut, V. C. (2010). Diversity science: Why and how difference makes a difference. *Psychological Inquiry, 21*, 77–99. doi: 10.1080/10478401003676501

Chapter 3

Understanding Cultural Humility and Civility

"Treat me beyond what you see and the encounters you've had with others who look like me. Get to know me, as I continue my journey of self-discovery and understanding. Learn what shapes me and uncover what we have in common. And while you do that for me, I will commit to doing the same for you. See my identities as a reflection of who I am, not what I am, and even when we don't agree, respect the humanity in me. Understand the story behind my personality. And when we have reached a level of competence, let's do it all over again. There's bound to be a new experience, a new idea, a new reality yet realized and understood."

—Candice Dowd Barnes

The introduction depicts the essence of the intersection between cultural humility and civility. Humans are hardwired to draw explanations about the world from their personal experiences. We all have the capacity to engage in cultural humility and civility. Yet, the overwhelming question that challenges everyone is:

1) Will we risk our comfortable identities to engage in such a practice?

Perhaps the greater risk is forfeiting the chance to invest in humanity and allowing one's bias boundaries and identity protectionism or reluctance to expand understanding to steal away the ability to free oneself from ignorance. Perhaps it is the fear of the unknown or acknowledging the true narrative that someone shares about themselves that contradicts the bias boundaries and other-izing narratives about people. Perhaps it is simply an exercise in cultural humility that will allow one to answer the question or engage in such a practice.

First, let us explore the background and history of cultural humility in more detail. Later in the chapter, a brief discussion of civility will continue to set the stage for a discussion on the intersection of both cultural humility and civility, along with some reflection questions to guide one's thinking about the implication of the concepts more broadly.

THE ORIGINS OF CULTURAL HUMILITY

Cultural humility rose to prominence within the medical, nursing, and mental health disciplines. In those fields, the idea behind cultural humility was that the patient's outcomes are better when their treatments are created and adapted with cultural considerations guiding those treatments (Owen, Tao, Drinane, Hook, & Kune, 2015). This concept is quickly becoming a prominent theory in professions that arguably place a high value on the importance of multicultural competence and relationships. Most recently, cultural humility has found a place in other disciplines like education and the social sciences.

In many ways, cultural humility addresses the need to understand humanity and embrace the concept of self-renewal and discovery. In education, engaging in cultural humility can be a highly effective tool. Those in racially diverse school settings, for example, and those educators who work with students from dissimilar backgrounds and belief systems can greatly benefit from engaging in cultural humility that will undoubtedly lead to civility. Just imagine how effective teachers, leaders, and other school personnel could be if they systematically influenced the school's culture by engaging in a process that would allow people to interact based on authentic understandings and not assumptions about who those people are.

DEFINING CULTURAL HUMILITY

Humility across literature is defined in many ways. The definition the authors of this book have adopted is that humility is freedom from ignorance.

However, the authors expanded that definition to describe humility as also freedom of assumptions and the acidic commentary that has the propensity to erode humanity. When one adds the nuances of culture, race, and ethnicity, the breadth and depth of humility changes.

Humility, in general, has been the topic of social research for some time. It is considered a personality trait that one can possess as well as a character strength one might develop (Peters, Rowatt & Johnson, 2011). It is also considered a crucial piece of strong, sound relationships because people who are humble are more likely to empathize and practice patience. These are good traits to have when we are discussing differences. For example, if a person is interacting with others who are different from them, that they do not understand, and that they do not agree with on all levels, then one might need to practice humility, and thus, cultural humility is subordinate to the larger character trait of humility.

Cultural humility is a lifelong process of discovery that includes three primary elements—*awareness, sensitivity,* and *responsiveness*—which encourages individuals to engage in self-evaluation, reflection, and critique (Foronda, Baptiste, Reinholdt, & Ousman, 2016; Juarez et al., 2006). Cultural humility is beyond the scope of multicultural competence. It is highlighted by a sense of openness, curiosity, and a genuine desire to understand how other people live their lives. Therefore, the concept of cultural humility is deeper than just competence or proficiency. With cultural humility, no one assumes competence. Rather, an individual works to gain an understanding of who the other person is and how they see themselves (Owen et al., 2015).

Overall, cultural humility is characterized by understanding self and others to gain a better sense of how to collaborate, interact, and behave in a genuine way with each other. The idea is that one should strive to always engage in cultural humility across the lifespan because each new experience affirms or challenges one's thinking. Therefore, a person is never fully competent or developed because culture is always evolving and changing, and each day brings new experiences and learning. This is acutely true in education, where students come to school under the guise of learning—and learning can be academic, social, and cultural.

It is that desire to learn that may cause students to challenge, question, or come into conflict with other's thinking, action, and behavior. Learning occurs in and out of the classroom, and sometimes, it comes with emotional and physical responses that may or may not create conflict or contention. When individuals engage in cultural humility, they come into a space with an understanding that they may encounter some conflicts and challenges. They may be more prepared for those challenges because they know whom they are and if they are willing to learn about other individuals who are sharing the same space. Let us take a deeper look into the three elements of cultural humility—awareness, sensitivity, and responsiveness.

AWARENESS OF SELF AND OTHERS

In his book *Highly Effective People*, Steven Covey (1990) is known for suggesting, "seek first to understand before being understood." This is the basic premise for awareness. Awareness is a concept that indicates that one needs to take inventory of who they are and are becoming, and how that relates to others around them. If a person is not aware of his or her biases, that person cannot challenge beliefs that are maladaptive and potentially damaging.

One of the major characteristics of cultural humility is self-discovery and self-renewal. This suggests a continued and ongoing process of learning more about who you are as you grow and evolve. This process also guides one's experiences, values, affinity circles, and our thinking. It is also driven by a curiosity to engage more deeply in finding commonalities—ways in which people's lives might connect and opportunities to share ones lived and loved experiences.

Ultimately, once you become more aware of who you are and who other people are beyond the assumptions and characterizations you may have placed on them, the way you think about self and others will change. Your scope of understanding broadens, and your ability to make connections deepens. Awareness influences the ways in which one can begin to build an effective culture and connection in the classroom. Therefore, when, and if, a conflict arises, or a climatic shift occurs, the culture can withstand the impact.

SENSITIVITY TO SELF AND OTHERS

Sensitivity has an interesting etymology. The origin is related to the sensations of the soul. Humanity has not strayed far from the original meaning of sensitivity. To engage in sensitivity, in more contemporary terms, generally reflects a deep and intense feeling of something, circumstance, or someone. It might also suggest perspective-taking, which helps one engage in empathy. It is the expression and focus on empathy, which is the key to conflict recovery. Therefore, to be sensitive is to have a deeper and more purposeful consciousness of self and others. It also means that as your thinking deepens so too does your level of sensitivity and empathy.

Sensitivity is a critical factor for teacher effectiveness and school success. Social and cultural sensitivity remains an important element in understanding self and others and the ways in which one reflects on those experiences. Social sensitivity and cultural sensitivity in education are vital to helping build a space for recovery and restoration. In this regard, sensitivity addresses how behavior is shaped by thinking, and that leads to the way in which one engages in conflict recovery.

RESPONSIVENESS TO SELF AND OTHERS

Responsiveness is characterized by how one's thinking and behavior influences their actions. For the purposes of this book, actions are defined as advocacy, activities, investigations, questioning, tasks—the intentional steps toward a greater good or to resolve conflict satisfactorily. Simply put, determining how one serves self and others is the underpinning of responsiveness.

In this context, responsiveness reflects how one uses the information they know about someone else and themselves to respond appropriately and effectively to their needs. Conflict recovery speaks to how we investigate to understand and collect data to address the conflict more comprehensively. Therefore, how one responds is directly connected to the way in which someone is offered recovery.

Responsiveness also means that time is afforded to deploy various strategies to ensure one really understands someone else's perspective, and again, without making assumptions about who someone is or how their experiences have shaped their behaviors and thinking. They might have more opportunities to make decisions, provide necessary supports and resources, and to do so with respect and dignity. The overall idea is that when one engages in cultural humility it makes it easier to engage with others in a civil manner. Therefore, by engaging each aspect of cultural humility fosters the ability to be empathetic and patient. It also creates the space for civility to grow.

CIVILITY

There is an appreciable civility crisis across local, national, and global communities. Civility is a hot button issue that has permeated our politics, workplace and school environments, and our respective communities. There are fewer and fewer examples of people exercising civility, and the overall public, in general, is failing to engage in civility. Schools are also experiencing incivility at alarming rates. Unfortunately, civility, for all of the hope that it brings, sometimes viewed quite negatively.

Civility has become so polarizing that many individuals are retreating from interactions, relationships, and debates because they fear being called out for being uncivil or any other negative term that it can sometimes be synonymous with incivility (i.e., racist, sexist, homophobic, etc.). Why does the word "civility" invoke such negativity? One answer might be the attitudes by those in authority who continually accuse others of being uncivil when they themselves practicing incivility.

In recent social media posts and online literature, civility has become a sledgehammer designed to challenge the better angels in people. In some instances, civility is dishonored through aggressive rhetoric and behavior. In a recent speech at the University of Illinois, where former president Barack Obama was receiving an award, he shared his thoughts on the state of civility in America. While his statement focused on politics, his comments were an example of how civility is defined by the current context in which we live.

President Obama encouraged the audience to move away from the idea of being polite, so long as you get what you want. He furthered his disdain for incivility by drawing attention to the abdication of one's responsibility to act when they witness incivility, and to do more to bring attention to those in positions of power who exercise incivility (Politico, 2018).

UNDERSTANDING THE DECLINE OF CIVILITY

For the past ten years, Weber-Shandwick has produced the *Civility in America* report. These reports have presented a sobering picture of Americans' experiences with incivility or uncivil behavior in greater numbers. For example, more than 60 percent of people who participated in the 2017 survey reported incivility leads to harassment, violence, and other types of threatening behavior. In that same survey, participants overwhelmingly reported they are civil but also indicated that in general people in the United States are uncivil, taking little to no responsibility for being a part of the problem themselves (Weber-Shandwick, 2017).

In fact, Gaines-Ross (2017) reported that one-quarter of Americans have left their jobs because of incivility and claim intimidation, harassment, and in some instances, violence and discrimination as some of the more serious ramifications of incivility. However, incivility is not relegated to the workplace; it is also quite prevalent in educational systems across the country.

Since 2010, parents have reported their children are experiencing more incivility in schools and neighborhoods (Weber-Shandwick, 2016). Numerous videos of incivility demonstrated in our schools can be found on various social media outlets. Incidents of incivility in communities spill over into our schools and classrooms, frequently. Within schools, incidents and conflicts between teachers and students, student to student, and colleague to colleague happen almost daily.

While it is a fact that individuals might experience incivility throughout their lifetimes, incivility should not be a normal experience. It should not become society's new normal. The way in which we interact with each other through social media and across our cultural diaspora is arguably disheartening. It is a betraying of the decency in humanity when one engages in incivility.

INCIVILITY IN TODAY'S WORLD

Generally, there are three primary reasons why these authors believe there has been a decline in civility throughout and across various groups. One, there is a lack of cultural humility. The inability to expand thinking, actions, and behaviors to broaden the context by which one interacts and engages with others in an authentic way. When one engages in the lifelong process of self-discovery and learning about others, they are essentially exercising cultural humility and applying cultural capital to deepen their understanding of social norms and the status of individuals. New experiences will then shape and mold one's thinking, action, and behaviors toward self and others.

Two, incivility in systematic structures such as politics has strained and challenged many social and cultural ideologies related to equity and inclusion. Thus leading to a resurgence of false narratives and disenfranchising beliefs about marginalized groups of people. This coupled with the social and cultural ideologies embedded within the current U.S. political administration, for instance, is greatly affecting how people engage and interact with each other nationally and internationally.

Three, technology has made it easier to disengage from society and to engage in bullying and represent civility as no more than cordial commentary. It is commonly known that cyberbullying has led to some life-altering incidents. While organizations, schools, and higher education institutions provide employees and students with email etiquette workshops and protocols to help stem the tide of incivility behind the computer screen, the problem persists.

For all the wonderful evolutionary advantages that technology has provided society with, technology has also caused new challenges in how people interact with respect and decency toward one another. Therefore, there must be a change in the narrative and the context in which we define, discuss, and teach civility.

REIMAGING CIVILITY

For the purposes of this discussion, civility is defined as thinking, actions, and behaviors the respects and values humanity. This reframing or reimaging of civility is key to understanding the larger, broader underpinnings of cultural humility. Civility is often described and defined as niceties, gestures, please and thank you, and so on. However, when you reimagine what civility sounds like, feels like, and the actions you might take to exhibit civility, the way in which you internalize the term changes.

Civility is not just about being polite, nice, or thoughtful. It is how one demonstrates compassion, courage, and kindness. It is the ways in which an individual reflects these ideas and attributes in his her daily practices and interactions. It is the way in which one might help someone in need, acknowledge their beliefs, engage in understanding, and allow someone to understand who they are. When you engage in deep cultural humility, it will lead to civility, and that is bookended by respect and personality. And civility is a much needed character trait in school's today. A deeper discussion of the intersection between cultural humility and civility and the importance of both in education will be presented in chapter 4.

FINAL THOUGHTS

In closing, there are multiple and varied ways that civility and cultural humility can make one's interactions more productive. Understanding that the concept of civility reaching depths beyond gesturing, politeness, or manners can go a long way in how individuals seek to understand each other. The next chapter will provide an overview of the discussion of cultural humility in education and will offer some activities to help engage in conversations about our identities and affinity groups—all in an effort to build and cultivate high-performance relationships and decrease the incidence of conflict.

THINK, REFLECT, CONNECT

1. Think back to an experience in which you displayed cultural humility while interacting with someone. How did this impact the interaction? If the interaction developed into a relationship, how did trust between the parties involved strengthen?
2. The authors have shared their opinions on why incivility is spreading at a rapid pace today. Can you think of any other reasons for such incivility that you could add to the authors list of reasons? Why are those additions central to your professional practices or personal experiences? Which one of the author's reasons for increased incivility have you experienced recently?
3. Reframing civility beyond known definitions and descriptions was presented earlier. How does this reimaged description resonate with you? What are some examples where you have demonstrated this reimaged description of civility in your personal and professional life?

_____
_____
_____
_____

REFERENCES

Covey, S. (1990). *The seven habits of highly effective people: Powerful lessons in personal change.* New York, NY: Free Press Publishing.

Foronda, C., Baptiste, D. L., Reinholdt, M. M., & Ousman, K. (2016). Cultural humility: A concept analysis. *Journal of Transcultural Nursing, 23*(7), 210–17. doi: 10.1177/1043659615592677

Gaines-Ross, L. (2017, June 18). *Incivilization.* Retrieved from https://www.linkedin.com/pulse/incivilization-2017-leslie-gaines-ross

Juarez, J. A., Marvel, K., Brezinski, K. L., Glazner, C., Towbin, M. M., & Lawton, S. (2006). Bridging the gap: A curriculum to teach residents cultural humility. *Family Medicine, 38*(2), 97–102.

Owen, J., Tao, K. W., Drinane, J. M., Hook, J., Davis, D. E., & Kune, N. F. (2015). Client perceptions of therapists' multicultural orientation: Cultural (missed) opportunities and cultural humility. *Professional Psychology: Research and Practice, 47*(1), 1–8. doi: http://dx.doi.org/10.1037/pro0000046

Peters, A. S., Rowatt, W. C., & Johnson, M. K. (2011). Associations between dispositional humility and social relationship quality. *Psychology, 2*(3), 155–61. doi: 10.4236/psych.2011.23025

Politico. (2018). Transcript: Former President Obama's speech at the University of Illinois. Retrieved from https://www.politico.com/story/2018/09/07/obama-university-of-illinois-speech-811130

Weber-Shandwick. (2017). Civility in America 2017: Political edition. Retrieved from https://www.webershandwick.com/news/poll-finds-americans-united-in-seeing-an-uncivil-nation-divided-about-cause/

Chapter 4

The Need for Cultural Humility and Civility in Education

"To share your weakness is to make yourself vulnerable; to make yourself vulnerable is to show your strength."

—Criss Jami

Cultural humility sounds commonsensical; however, the quote above epitomizes what humility and cultural humility truly is. It is a sense of vulnerability of self and the knowledge of others. It is a shift away from an overrepresentation of expertise to an acknowledgement that learning is ongoing, culture is ever-changing, and humility is key to ensuring a real understanding of self and others and to use that information to effectively serve others in need. It is the essence of the elements of cultural humility—awareness, sensitivity, and responsiveness.

In order to provide a person with appropriate care, compassion, dignity, respect, or civility, you might actually need to know who they are and how they present themselves to the world. As the concept of cultural humility grows in education, it can speak to how effectively a school or classroom culture of respect is built and managed. It might also guide how leaders, teachers, students, counselors, and others interact with each other effectively. Cultural humility in education can address how one's thinking, action, and behavior can drive the way in which individuals offer each other grace (recovery) and restoration when conflicts occur.

In this chapter, the authors will focus on three primary concepts to support the need for cultural humility and civility in education and will depict the intersection of civility and cultural humility. This chapter will also reckon with the concept of protectionism and identity-protective cognition. In the next section, a theoretical framework offers a suggested developmental process that might explain how one cycles through cultural humility and the level where most people plateau. The chapter will end with a think, reflect, connect section to aid the reader in focusing on practices and actions to help implement the concepts effectively.

A DEVELOPMENTAL CYCLE FOR CULTURAL HUMILITY

The authors suggest that engaging in cultural humility affords one the opportunity to cycle through Kegan's developmental process, as suggested by Puchner & Markowitz (2016), with the goal of achieving proficiency or competency in certain aspects, while constantly adding to one's understanding. Kegan's model consists of four stages that people can cycle through to make a meaning about the realities around them.

Puchner & Markowitz (2016) used this model to help explain why it is hard for teachers to understand how racism manifests. While the authors are not focused on racism, a parallel can be made to explain how individuals understand each other and themselves. Certainly, race can be central to that understanding. The stages are identified below.

1) No distinction of self, perceptions, and impulses. This is generally an early development stage.
2) No separation of self from feelings and objects. As one develops, one also experiences the world through their own lens and perspective.
3) Abstract thinking and reflection of one's own beliefs and values. This is a more developed stage where an in-depth understanding begins to materialize.
4) Develop a life that acknowledges where their values conflict with others thinking, action, and behavior.

They argue that most adults never reach level four and tend remain in levels two or three, which are about self and others. These early levels can be aligned with identity protectionism which will be discussed later. For now, the realization that adaptation will be a necessary part of the continual growth process is an essential step for people to reach level four.

Cultural humility and awareness could be an avenue that allows teachers to move through the developmental levels; however, this happens along a continuum, or maybe, in a cyclical fashion where an individual enters and exits competency and proficiency as they add to their current understanding. Sound complicated?

Not really, it is how we consume life—in cycles of experiences and occurrences. It is how we explore our own and understand other people have lived, loved, and longed experiences. Therefore, as we cycle in and out of new experiences, store memories, and use our knowledge about those experiences as benchmarks for the forthcoming experiences. We are essentially moving in and out or back and forth through cultural development, and we are building our cultural IQ.

Consider this: Sarah is a school counselor working in a predominantly minority school. The students view her as other, and although she is trained to counsel and recognize students in need, she is challenged by their vernacular and gesturing. It is very unfamiliar to her own experiences and culture. She is concerned that she has nothing in common with these students and cannot connect with them.

In this scenario, Sarah and her students have engaged in assumptions about each other that could hinder their ability to engage in healthy interactions and high-engaged relationships. High-engagement relationships will be discussed in detail in chapter 5, as it relates to the teacher; however, it generally involves belonging, accountability, and recovery.

CULTURALISM AND IDENTITY-PROTECTIVE COGNITION

Countless research studies have examined the implication of race and culturalism in schools. Studies have stressed the notion that students, in particular, are often misjudged or mischaracterized simply because of the implicit and conscious bias of their teachers and other school personnel. There are also studies that assert these biases begin in young students' early childhood years (Pauker, Ambady, & Apfelbaum, 2010).

This can be quite problematic and influence the way in which groups of people interact, build relationships, understand different communication styles, or even how to engage in recovery and restorative practices when conflicts occur. There is often a false narrative projected about *culturalism* in education—a notion that educators are naturally culturally responsive, or should be more culturally responsive because they work with diverse populations of students.

In some instances, that is, unfortunately, quite the opposite. Educators, like all humans, are bound by their biases, which are based on their values, beliefs, backgrounds, and experiences. Depending on the narrow scope of experiences with others of dissimilar backgrounds, or just the sheer lack of exposure to challenging thoughts and ideas, these groups can quickly engage in conflict based on assumptions and generalizations.

When individuals foster cultural humility and civility, it provides them opportunities to engage in cultural conflict recovery and restorative practices that allow for meaningful discourse, discussions, and actions that do not label people as simply "the other." This can be especially important in education where people can often misjudge and can be misjudged because of their backgrounds, histories, identities, and values. Allowing mischaracterizations of other people can lead to some negative and detrimental effects in the classroom, school, and greater community.

Therefore, it is imperative that individuals find a richer, more meaningful way to learn about other people without other-izing them. The grand goal is to understand the intersectionality and commonalities in each other's lives so that those experiences and ways of being can be embraced, celebrated, and recognized. This can happen even if individuals do not come into agreement or have conflicts about other people's lived and loved experiences. It is about forming an understanding that each and every individual you encounter has a personal narrative that is unique to them and should not always be generalized to others.

When you embrace the idea that there are more meaningful ways to engage, then one can push back or push down their bias boundaries, the need for uncompromising identity protectionism, and the negative assumptions about others that may or may not be true. Ultimately, the goal is to respect the humanity that lives in all people and gain a greater insight into how their personality shapes their being, thereby embracing civility and cultural humility as more than social propaganda, but a way of living.

INTERSECTION OF CULTURAL HUMILITY AND CIVILITY IN EDUCATION

Culture alone is complex because there is no single definition of culture. A person's culture can be any aspect that is salient to them as an individual. Culture, therefore, is important for relationships where there is a power differential, such as in a client-therapist relationship or a student-teacher relationship. When a person is culturally humble, they are less likely to miss opportunities to learn about a person's culture and values. They are more likely to take advantage of a meaningful relationship, which creates connection and relatedness.

Therefore, educators who are working to develop meaningful alliances between him or herself and his or her students increase opportunities to affect the educational outcomes and make greater investments in the humanity represented in their classrooms. It also creates space for the school personnel to examine and explore their biases about each other and the respective groups with which they, the student and teacher, identifies. As discussed before, these conversations alone help promote an understanding of each other as individuals and increases the chances that the interaction will remain civil.

Bonds, mutual goals, and collaborative tasks support a greater understanding of the aspects that are salient to the person's culture characterize strong alliances (Hook, Davis, Owen, & DeBlaere, 2017). Having conversations about culture and differences that are evident can go a long way toward improving those alliances and relationships. According to the National Center for Cultural Competence (2004), awareness and knowledge are developmental processes that are constantly evolving throughout both individual and organizational life spans. Needs and the level of support will be different for every individual, which is why it is important to understand their perspective on various cultural issues, even if the topic or rhetoric is vastly different from your own.

When we are engaging in cultural humility, we apply the elements of responsiveness, awareness, and sensitivity to how one thinks, acts, and behaves, as suggested in figure 1. When one makes those elements a part of their daily practices, it is more likely that the interactions and encounters with other people will occur with civility. Civility, as defined by the authors, is how thinking, action, and behavior respects and values humanity, and civility is bookended by respect and personality. The intersection of both cultural humility and civility is depicted in figure 1. (See figure 1).

The way in which one understands and feels respect is defined by their knowledge, experiences, interactions, and relationships with others. Respect is a value that should be practiced daily. It should be a part of what we do, and should demonstrate to others what we think of ourselves and how we value them. Additionally, when one demonstrates respect they are communicating to the person that they care and acknowledge their history, backgrounds, and narratives.

Personality, then, allows for the authenticity in communication, interactions, and encounters. Personality is driven by the person's bias boundaries—their values and beliefs that shape who they are and how they interact with their world. It is deeper than persona which is how we represent ourselves to the world. When your personality is mistaken for your persona, that may have a negative effect on one's ability to engage the elements of cultural humility or civility. Therefore, making purposeful decisions to show your most genuine self when interacting can cultivate fertile soil for high-performance, high-engaged relationships to develop.

Let us examine the following scenario to bring a deeper understanding of the intersection of cultural humility and civility.

A group of twenty white, female teacher education candidates who share similar conservative-Christian, middle-class, rural values, are suddenly thrust into a student teaching experience with predominantly African American students, (mostly male), from middle-class families, whose values are based in Islamic and Black Liberation theology.

What could go wrong? Where will there be a disconnect? What conversations need to be had?

In this scenario, while both groups share the same social class, even that may look dramatically different depending on a multitude of circumstances and situations. Additionally, neither the teacher candidates nor the students are prepared for the discussion style conflicts that will surely arise.

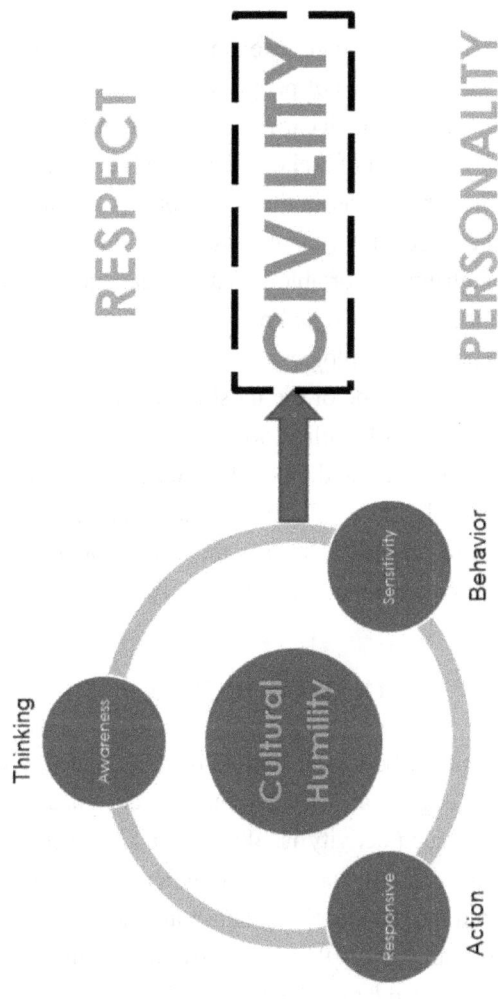

Figure 1

Each person involved in this scenario, if provided the space to genuinely engage in cultural humility, could learn about each other's individual thinking, beliefs, values, and experiences that can potentially strip away the power differentials and the betrayal of authenticity—the representation of who you want to be, not who you are. This allows the opportunity for a civil exchange of beliefs where the teachers engage in understanding, and the students feel heard and vice versa.

Otherwise, this scenario could be an example of the perfect storm to grow deeper dissension among groups of people who will occupy the same physical space for months. It is through earnest cultural humility that one can truly begin to attempt the heavy lift of racial and cultural inequity and tension. The teacher, as an instructional leader in the classroom, is also the agent of social change for his or her students in many ways. And those teachers must lead their students through uncomfortable situations and difficult conversations that will challenge their deeply rooted patterns of thinking and behaving, and their cultural identities and ideologies.

The authors propose that one of the most effective ways to foster conflict recovery is through cultural humility, which will then lead to civility. Once an individual understands self and others by engaging in an ongoing process of self-renewal, that individual will undoubtedly behave, think, and act in a more civil manner toward others. That is the essence and true nature of the intersection between cultural humility and civility.

FINAL THOUGHTS

In closing, throughout the book, the authors plan to challenge you to answer tough questions and engage in activities that are designed to be thoughtful and meaningful. One such activity is, *What's on Your Table?* This activity can be used as a conversation starter, dialogue enhancer, or a way to share and discuss perspectives, assumptions, and realities of one's identities and experiences. It is also an activity that can assist one in entering into, and exiting from, conversations that leave all parties with a sense of acknowledgment and validation. This is vital to conflict recovery. Conflict recovery will be discussed in detail in chapter six.

The authors suggest that when you engage in the *What's on Your Table* activity, you should focus on race, gender, and a combination of a few identities that someone might find out after one or two conversations. After having participants write those identifies in the respective circles, you might then allow them the opportunity to share others' assumptions about those identities, the way in which they characterize their identities, and perhaps, time and situation in which those identities were challenged or affirmed in some way. Below is a template, (figure 2), and an example of how you might facilitate this activity.

Activity instructions:

- Write down the identified characteristics that correspond with each circle.
- For the third circle, write as many identifying characteristics as possible according to the descriptors provided. Add more if you would like.
- Discuss at least one assumption about each of your identities.
- Discuss how YOU characterize your identities.
- Share a story or situation that challenged and affirmed your identities. Why?

WHAT'S ON YOUR TABLE?

Another activity that can be useful when attempting to engage in cultural humility and civility is *"So, WHO do you think I am?"* This activity is highly effective with students and can be used as an icebreaker for teacher development workshops. The idea is to present students, for example, with a set of questions about you. It is a simple activity that can be lighthearted way for students to see you as human. Below are some sample questions to consider. (See figure 3).

THINK, REFLECT, CONNECT

1) What are some ways in which you see cultural humility represented in your school or where might cultural humility and civility be effective?
2) How could you make an investment to facilitate activities like *What's on Your Table* help you to change your school's ethos—the cultural spirit based on beliefs and values?
3) How does protectionism impact your ability to interact and engage with your colleagues, students, and others about seemingly uncomfortable and difficult issues?

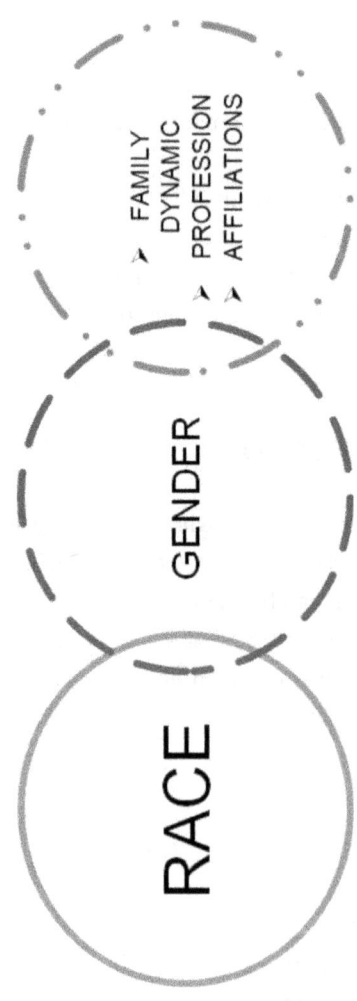

Figure 2

```
┌─────────────────────────────────────────────────────────┐
│                 So, WHO do you think I Am?              │
│  Where do you think I was born and raised?              │
│  What do you think I like to do for fun?                │
│  What type of pet do you think I'd have?                │
│  What do you think is my favorite type of movie?        │
│  What's my favorite series on Netflix?                  │
│  Where was my favorite field trip as a child?           │
└─────────────────────────────────────────────────────────┘
```

Figure 3

4) Which of the three elements of cultural humility might require the most work in order for you to feel confident in your ability to engage in deeper equity and inclusion?
5) What recent situations come to mind that affirms or challenges the idea that cultural competency and proficiency is limited in scope, and cultural humility provides a broader view of how one's lived and loved experiences shape their lives?

_____
_____
_____
_____
_____

REFERENCES

Department of Education (2016). *The state of racial diversity in the educator workforce* (pp. 5–6). Washington, DC.

Ford, T. N. & Quinn, L. (2010). First-year teachers education candidates: What are their perceptions about multicultural education? *Multicultural Education, 17*(4), 18–24.

Chapter 5

Making the Change

> *"Incredible change happens in your life when you decide to take control of what you do have power over instead of craving control over what you don't."*
>
> —*Steve Maraboli*

In this chapter, the authors discuss the perspective that one might consider expanding their understanding beyond competency and proficiency. While this type of thinking is key, that is not to say that one should abandon ideas like cultural competency and proficiency. For example, it might be that one will eventually achieve proficiency in a cultural element and during a specific time.

However, to assert that one is competent in something that is constantly changing, evolving, and integrating, is naive. The key is recognizing the limitations of proficiency and recognizing that each person is their own individual with their own identities and true competence is not possible. Cultures can change and be influenced by other cultures, and are, therefore, fluid in nature and we must be willing to learn and make adjustments at all times.

This chapter will also discuss training and professional development as a way to help educators make the shift toward cultural humility by changing the language and engaging in meaningful actions to make cultural humility a normalized practice. Most importantly, the training is a shift away from the thinking that one might reach an endpoint of cultural competence. Culture changes and shifts with every generation and is nuanced as people grow and learn new ideas and new ways of being. Therefore, there is no endpoint, no sense of competency.

When educational reform is discussed, the discussion will create feelings of uneasiness. There is often this type of sinking feeling because the discussion generally means a new project, initiative, or curriculum will be introduced. It's the initiativitis syndrome defined in the glossary of terms. It is also uncomfortable because it generally means that some type of change might occur and change can be difficult. However, in order to experience desired results, it might mean that one is uncomfortable.

It also means that the change one seeks will take time. In other words, to achieve the results quickly, you might be uncomfortable. If you sacrifice comfort, then the results you seek will take time. Considering your approach, you have to be intentional and purposeful about how you move forward and how you measure progress. This is also true of implementing cultural humility and civility into practice. It is what the authors refer to as the paradigm of innovation—in order to see the results—the change you desire, you will have to compromise time or comfort.

Think about the last time you tried to make a change in your own personal life and reflect on how and what informed that decision to make the change. Maybe the decision was to start a diet, purchase a big-ticket item, or decide if following your GPS directions is a good idea. Change will happen whether welcomed or not. There is an old saying, "nothing is constant but change." Everything around us is in a constant state of change.

This certainly applies to culture—and cultural changes and shifts are inevitable in education. There is no doubting that. The social and cultural changes, demographic changes, and such, must be attended to so that educators are sensitive and responsive to the needs of their community of learners. This is necessary when setting, building, or creating sustainable school or classroom culture—a culture where humility, not competency, is king.

THE SHIFT FROM COMPETENCY TO HUMILITY

The traditional model for diversity training has been a competency model. It is based on the idea that once trained on the topic of diversity, which might include defining diversity and other related concepts you might learn from a book, that means you have been sufficiently and officially trained to interact with people from dissimilar backgrounds. It is actually quite the opposite.

What tends to happen is those who have participated in the training take that information and categorize or generalize what they learned to an entire group of people. Certainly, there are some cultural similarities that people who identify with the same group has, but that is not always true. A better way is to think about diversity training from a cultural humility standpoint.

Otherwise, one might be sending the wrong signal or engage in training that will create a greater divide or a false response. This false response to diversity training is a concept that the authors addressed in earlier chapters. It is the sense that one has reached a level of proficiency and that information stands as a gold standard instead of understanding that culture is fluid. Therefore, the need, imperatively, shifts from a narrow focus to a broader perspective of equity and inclusion. This type of shift in thinking is most substantial when it starts with cultural humility, first.

The *Cultural Competence Continuum* as presented by the National Center for Cultural Competence. This organization highlights six steps along this continuum: (1) cultural destructiveness, (2) cultural incapacity, (3) cultural blindness, (4) cultural pre-competence, (5) cultural competency, and (6) cultural proficiency (Goode, 2004).

While the authors of this book highlight competence and proficiency, it is apparent that awareness of and examining one's own assumptions, prejudices, and stereotypes is the first step to positive learning and interacting with one another. As one cycles through this cultural competence continuum as described above, it is likely that one might also be reaching deeper developmental levels, as suggested by Kegan.

However, the authors of this book reiterate that as one continues the cycle, you also pick up new bits of information that changes and deepens your resolve. This information may also help you examine yourself and understand others. So, again, it's not an abandoning of competence and proficiency completely, but a different way to think about what competence means from a cultural perspective. Let us take a deeper look into the concepts of cultural competence and proficiency.

COMPETENCE AND PROFICIENCY

Competence is a demonstration of acceptance and respect for cultural differences (Goode, 2004). This stage involves implementing culturally appropriate and evidence-based practices, developing strategies that incorporate community involvement, and engaging in training to increase an individual's levels of cultural competence (Goode, 2004). This is an important framing when training because it pulls on the string of respect, which is key to the intersection of cultural humility and civility.

Cultural proficiency is when an individual or an organization holds culture and diversity in high esteem, and it is a foundation of the individual or the system (Goode, 2004). This stage involves continuing to add to a knowledge base, and conducting research to develop approaches, adopting an organizational philosophy and practices that support culture (Goode, 2004). This way of thinking about proficiency aligns more with the authors' suggestion that cultural humility and civility should be at the forefront and not proficiency. This way of thinking about proficiency essentially entails consistency and consciously adds to what is known and understood.

The assumption with most understood definitions of competence and proficiency is that there is an end goal. However, there is no final destination toward cultural humility. By engaging in cultural humility, there is always room for continual growth, even when an individual or organization arrives at the competency or the proficiency stage in a specific area. Humility, however, helps us to expand and adapt as culture does.

Competency and proficiency have a finality that humility does not. Culture, by nature, is never culminated. Therefore, the continuous desire to engage in learning about oneself and others will only serve to deepen the relationship, understanding, and respect for others. This process of cultural humility, at its core, involves continual self-evaluation, critique, and self-discovery. Cultural humility could be a catalyst for moving along the competence continuum, especially in a highly diverse school setting.

It is essential to create a culture of learning in the classroom where viewpoints, even polarizing viewpoints, are heard, and the humanity of the individual is respected. It is critical to make a shift in thinking to best meet the needs of the students you come into contact with. This change needs to start in degree programs where future generation of teachers, administrators, or mental health professionals is trained. The importance of cultural humility and civility in higher education institutions will be discussed in detail in a later chapter. For now, let us discuss diversity training and professional development more generally.

THE IMPORTANCE OF TRAINING AND PROFESSIONAL DEVELOPMENT

Taking on a new way of thinking can be difficult. However, what the authors suggest is that you delve deeper into a practice that you have probably already engaged in, just on a more intentional level. There are so many different factors to consider when deciding to incorporate new ideas perspectives, language, concepts, and so on. Hence, why training can be a challenge, but is definitely necessary.

Most training, to be successful, requires the participants to buy-in to the process and understand the importance and purpose. Most importantly for diversity training, the questions that typically make or break strong and effective implementation are:

1. How is this going to change my students' behavior and actions?
2. How will this information confirm or deny what I already understand is the truth about a group of people?
3. What type of blame and shame will I have to endure as a result of this training?
4. What are the expectations, and what type of accountability will come with this new training?
5. How is this different from everything else I've attended?

Certainly, other questions arise when contemplating diversity training. These are just a sample. What the authors suggest is a different way to approach this type of training that starts with a conversation—a dialogue about the emotionality that all diversity training evokes. This would also include creating norms that allow participants to discuss their feelings and fears in a safe and a brave space. Hopefully, these spaces will allow for authentic relationships to grow. More training strategies and considerations will be presented later in this chapter.

When it comes to the classroom, teachers need to develop relationships with their students, but not be overly involved in their personal lives. This is the same for all school personnel. What the authors recommend is that a school's staff engage in training facilitated by experts and training that allows for dynamic role play, conversations, thinking, and action planning.

It is an approach, that when done with intentionality, can be successful and sustainable.

Training should not just focus on diversity, but should allow participants to ask questions, reflect upon the material presented, explore their potential biases, and focus on equity and inclusion implementation. The fact is most training programs are designed to only focus on a portion of these components, and teacher education programs do not generally have dedicated classes on racial diversity, multiculturalism, and certainly not, cultural humility can be problematic.

Some degree programs may have courses on diverse learners. Those courses are typically not about culture. For other teacher education programs, there may be courses that focus on all categories of diversity, but not necessarily on equity and inclusion. Likewise, professional development for practicing professionals is often geared toward academics and prescribed behavior intervention that rarely account for the ebb and flow of the humanity that exist across all schools.

This lack in substantive and quality training is leading to a relational gap between teachers and students because teachers are not trained to think about who their students are. They are trained to focus on what to teach their students. Therefore, the focus for most teacher education programs is academic content curriculum. There is less intensity placed on building relationships, or on how to teach students how to respect one another.

This is why cultural humility training is important in teacher education and for practicing professionals. The overarching focus of cultural humility is relational and a teacher—all educators—can serve their students better when they know who they are, and when they are sensitive to their needs and respond accordingly.

Once educators and other school personnel are practicing professionals, there is a significant need for them to be trained in cultural issues, especially if their programs of study did not provide adequate training or content. In fact, teachers are often not exposed to diversity training during their field placements. This is problematic because, as was discussed earlier, the demographics are changing. In highly diverse schools, where the staff is mostly white, this lack of cultural humility training can be a significant issue that leads to misinterpretation and misunderstandings about students of color.

Bloom and Peters (2012) examined white racial identity development and self-efficacy of teacher candidates and found that as teacher candidates had more contact with diverse students, their belief in their ability to effectively use instructional strategies, classroom management, and engaging students decreased (Bloom & Peters, 2012). This indicates that as the diversity of field placement, meaning more students of color, increases, the less effective teacher candidates felt toward utilizing instructional strategies and managing their classrooms.

Teacher education programs should help educators and other school personnel to be good teachers, leaders, and counselors, yes, and to also be effective and responsive professionals for all students without biases. A part of this requires educators to recognize their own personal biases and prejudices. This is extremely important for teachers and teacher candidates to be sensitive to and hyperaware of when interacting regularly with students of color.

This group of educators have to learn how to consider the perspectives of students who come from different backgrounds than them. They have to learn to see themselves as agents of social change, because they are the primary instructional facilitators in schools. Students have a variety of identities and teachers cannot superficially try to understand them with basic knowledge and generalizations. They must go deeper into themselves and make concerted efforts to understand the backgrounds, histories, and lives of their students. This would also include understanding the structural issues and the community challenges their students face daily.

Humans tend to view their own values, beliefs, and actions as the norm. And because most people have a romanticized view of diversity, that is mostly information and collected from folklore, those views become the bases for how the actions, behavior, and thinking of a group is understood. The amount of time educators, especially teachers, spend with students supports the ideas that those individuals engage in substantive and meaningful training that allows them to understand their students individually to best teach, counsel, and guide them.

The authors suggest that educators and preprofessional candidates need to be trained in the following areas as a part of their programs of study and for ongoing professional development.

- The history of race relations and the systemic and structural issues that make equity and inclusion a challenge for students of color.
- What to do as opposed to what not to do. A lot of diversity training focuses on the negative aspects that perpetuate blame and shame and does nothing

to train on how to improve relationships. Focusing on what individuals should do changes the tenor and temperature of diversity training.
- Acknowledging the beliefs and perspectives and engaging in an awareness of self—an element of cultural humility.
- Learn how to apply their observations and analytical skills to monitor, evaluate, and revise their own practices to avoid biases and microaggressions. This would include training on micro-affirmations—small, consistent positive words of encouragement and support.
- Practical and useful strategies to get to know their students individually and critically analyze their experiences, opportunities that help or hinder their abilities and capabilities.
- Engage in how to facilitate difficult conversations about difficult issues in the classroom and school. These conversations should not be loaded with blame or shame, but understanding, respect, and dignity.
- Learn how to engage students in service-learning projects to develop empathy and perspective taking, care and consideration of others. This can be critical to long-standing and internalized understanding of who people are beyond their identities.
- Engage in an in-depth understanding of cultural humility, civility, recovery, and restorative principles that can help create appropriate and positive behavior and academic success plans.

Clearly, no one wants to see themselves as having biases and so they often shy away from opportunities to address these biases. However, this practice is dangerous because not only is the individual not addressing biases, but also they are convincing themselves that they do not have biases. This thinking could lead to unconscious stereotyping and damaging behavior. Therefore, by engaging in cultural humility the individual is engaged in continual and intentional practice and learns through experiences and interactions over time that their students are multilayer individuals who need to be understood, accepted, and have a sense of belonging.

FINAL THOUGHTS

Change is difficult. It can be especially difficult when the proposed change involves an institution that is deeply designed for the success of the majority culture. It remains a system where resources, funding, and access are based on zip codes and economics. It is not easy to take an entire system and change it overnight; however, one can make small steps in the right direction.

There is a strong need for a shift from a traditional competency viewpoint to a view that is grounded in cultural humility. However, the authors believe that the teacher education programs and professional development could be a catalyst for the desired change toward greater humility, respect, dignity, and conflict recovery. Putting people in the field who are prepared to practice self-awareness and reflection, and who are willing to learn from their students and their families, will make a small step in the right direction. Teacher education programs are the spark that can light the fire of change, and once those candidates become practicing professional, they will need to continue to engage cultural humility and civility consistently.

THINK, REFLECT, CONNECT

1. Think about your degree program. Whether you are a teacher, administrator, or mental health professional. Think about the strengths of your program in addressing multicultural issues and the weaknesses. What could have been done better? How did you receive training in the area of self-reflection?
2. Think about a bias you have (and yes we all have them) and take a moment to write about a time that this bias has affected you. Was it in your teaching? At the mall? In a social environment? Dig deep into your thoughts and the actions that followed. How could a deep reflection and awareness of self help move your thinking and behaviors differently?
3. Thinking about your bias, brainstorm some ideas for how to handle this bias in the future. What can you do differently? How can you make sure you are aware in the future? Is there someone in your life with that identity with whom you can talk openly with?

_____
_____
_____
_____
_____

REFERENCES

Bloom, D. S. & Peters, T. (2012). Student teaching experiences in diverse settings, white racial identity development and teacher efficacy. *Journal of Educational and Development Psychology, 2*(2), 72–84. doi: 10.5539/jedp.v2n2p72

Goode, T. D. (2004). *Cultural competence continuum.* Retrieved from http://gucchd.georgetown.edu

Schuessler, J. B., Wilder, B., & Byrd, L. W. (2012). Reflective journaling and development of cultural humility in students. *Nursing Education Perspectives, 33*(2), 96–99. doi: 10.5480/1536-5026-33.2.96

Sharma, S. (2005). Multicultural education: Teachers' perceptions and preparations. *Journal of College Teaching and Learning, 2*(5), 53–64.

Section II

FOR THE CULTURE

IMPLEMENTING CONFLICT RECOVERY IN SCHOOLS

This section is comprised of four chapters. Chapters 6, 7, and 8 address the complexity of conflict recovery from the teacher, leader, and mental health professional perspective. Chapter 9 provides context for conflict recovery, cultural humility, and civility in higher education institution and presents a method for delivering or integrating these concepts into programs of study and college cultures. Woven throughout these chapters is a story about a fictitious school, Brookdale High. While the high school is fictitious, the realities, people, and experiences can be found in schools across the country.

The chapters will include activities and exercises to prime you to think about your own school and how this information can be used to inform your practices, policies, and overall school culture, hence, *For the Culture*. The last chapter, chapter 10, will bring the concepts together under three overarching themes: people, policies, and practices. Each theme will incorporate cultural humility and civility and the foundation.

Chapter 6

Teaching
Cultural Humility and Civility in the Classroom

> "The paradox of education is precisely this—that as one begins to become conscious one begins to examine the society in which he is being educated."
>
> —James Baldwin

Brookdale High is an under-resourced school in a mid-size, first-tier suburban community, right outside of a major metropolitan city. Brookdale, like all other schools in the area, experienced a demographic shift over the last several years. The population of the community is now majority-minority with the highest numbers of people identifying as either African (from Nigeria or Liberia), Latino, or Hispanic. Most of the families live paycheck to paycheck and a large number of families are naturalized citizens. A small number of families have members who are also undocumented.

Mrs. Thomas and Juan have been at odds since the beginning of school. It is now October, and she has reached the end of her patience threshold. Juan is always late for school. He rarely has his homework ready. He is always disengaged and seems to influence "bad behavior" from other students. She redirects his behavior much too often, and she often finds him to be quite disrespectful and disruptive.

Very rarely is he absent, but when he is, the classroom environment is much different. Mrs. Thomas has attempted to address her concerns with his parents. They don't seem to be receptive and do nothing to support her. She has tried everything she knows to develop a relationship with him. She's even gone back to her cultural competence training to seek guidance on how to open dialogue with students like Juan. *None of that is working. She doesn't know what to do.*

This is a familiar story that many teachers face. They are teaching in schools where they may, or may not, have shared experiences with their students. They may be frustrated by students' behavior and may not have a real understanding of who their students are behind all of their identities and personas. As one explores the concepts shared in this chapter, reflect on how the information might be impacted by engaging the elements of cultural humility.

In chapter 1, the authors provided a rationale, a case for why cultural humility and civility in education is important and necessary. In chapters 2, 3, and 4, the origins of cultural humility were discussed, the shift from competency to humility was explored, cultural humility was defined, and the intersection of cultural humility and civility was highlighted. In this chapter, the reader will explore cultural humility and civility from the classroom perspective.

This chapter will specifically focus on the myths about multiculturalism and cultural competence of teachers working with diverse populations of students. Finally, it will explore the importance of cultural humility, the development of high-engagement relationships, and will further explain the concept of conflict recovery. Before exploring the concept of high-performance relationships in education, let us first grapple with the idea that teachers, especially those working with students from diverse and marginalized groups, are culturally aware. This thought, that these teachers have high cultural IQ's and use multiculturalism to foster a sense of awareness and competence, is faulty and potentially harmful.

MULTICULTURALISM AND CULTURAL AWARENESS IN EDUCATION

Multiculturalism is one of the most complex components of human existence. The literature on cultural awareness and cultural humility suggests there is no way to completely understand another person's culture unless you are immersed in that culture for an extended period. Moreover, even when a person does exactly that—immerse themselves in a culture—they still must grapple with the fact that culture changes and evolves. Multiculturalism, therefore, is viewed in both positive and hostile ways depending on the group promoting the idea (Plaut, Thomas, Hurd & Romano, 2018).

Researchers have studied the concept of culture for a very long time, and as the world continues to diversify and change, culture will continue to be a construct to be studied and understood. Culture has become a major focus across fields in journals, books, classroom discussions, and so on. Many search for answers to help them understand cultures and serve individuals from different cultures. However, what if the answer is that one must continue to explore and engage, and there is no end to something that is evolving. This is, in part, why a deeper dive into the psychological implications of multiculturalism can feel like a threat to some individuals.

The authors of this book are not advocating disavowing cultural awareness, competence, or even multiculturalism. However, the authors advocate for new ideas and thoughts to be considered to what multicultural competence means, and to do so by integrating cultural humility into daily practices and conversations. The world brings new challenges that have not previously been faced. Intersections of cultural views that have not been experienced or expressed flood the diaspora of humanity. These intersections should be studied, explored, acknowledged, and validated. Cultural humility is a prime way to engage in such activities.

For example, what happens when political, social, cultural, and religious ideologies and identities are brought into a classroom environment? How do all of these identities interact, and how does the teacher manage the culture within the classroom to ensure positive and high-performance relationships happen? The teacher, who is rightfully viewed as the authority figure in the classroom, is responsible for setting a tone for strong social interactions, relationships, and understanding.

The issue, however, is when the teacher engages in actions and behaviors that demotivate positive interpersonal outcomes. When one considers the myth that teachers working in highly diverse schools are somehow culturally competent and conscious, that can be a recipe for discrimination, disengagement, and diminished opportunities for recovery and restoration. This can cause critical relationship failure and it is difficult to repair that type of brokenness within a school year.

Therefore, while one might have high cultural intelligence in one area, that does not mean that one should rest on those laurels. Additionally, there should be no assumption that one is competent and proficient and does not need to add more to their understanding of others. It is also dangerous to assume that what is learned about one person can be generalized for an entire group of people who have individual histories and narratives, even if those individual affiliate with similar identity groups. Those narratives and histories deserve more than hyper-invalidation simply because the narrative might make someone uncomfortable.

This is particularly true of those in schools who are exposed to a variety of personalities, stories, and histories daily. When not careful, this hyper-invalidation can manifest itself in critical and harmful ways. This is partly why it can be dangerous to make assumptions about a teacher's cultural intelligence.

Multiculturalism, therefore, serves populations of people in many ways and those understandings must be considered when attempting to create a space where positive relationships and interactions occur. Just the idea of multiculturalism can be seen as a threat to one's identity. More positively, it can be the thread to weave together the elements of cultural humility—sensitivity, awareness, and responsiveness—to engage positive interpersonal skills.

THE MYTHS ABOUT CULTURAL COMPETENCE IN DIVERSE SCHOOLS

There is a myth that teachers especially those working in diverse school settings are cultural aware—even competent. The authors of this book push against that narrative vehemently. The literature on this subject indicates that racial biases start in the early childhood years. It continues into the elementary grades and in special education where minority boys, in particular, are disproportionately overrepresented compared to others. More often than not, these groups of minority boys are placed in special education for perceived misbehavior, which might be unintentionally masking a lack of cultural humility between student and teacher.

Cultural barriers play a significant role in the determination of a student's behavior and academic performance. In fact, in a National Education Association's policy brief on disproportionality, the organization indicated this had been an issue for four decades, and minority students are often misidentified for special education. Again, emotional and behavioral issues are the primary reason why this particular demographic group is placed in special education. Some obvious questions are as follows:

1) What do these teachers know about their students?
2) How have students' cultural and linguistic backgrounds been considered?
3) How has the teacher examined his or her biases toward people of color that might be influencing their interaction and engagement with students of color?
4) How has the teacher created a relationship-driven space instead of a discipline-driven space?
5) What role might cultural humility play in this, and similar types of instances, where bias is present?

This particular issue of overrepresentation of minorities in special education will not be reviewed extensively in this book. It will be used as a rhetorical example to highlight significant challenges across our K–12 classrooms, where teachers and students have great difficulty building relationships and bonds that might positively influence the student's academic success and social and emotional learning.

This is why the authors believe that embracing the ways in which individuals understand each other is critical to not only fostering good citizenship among students, but providing them a platform to build global, local, and national discourse and communities to be true influencers of change. But how? The next section offers considerations that do not discard the idea of multiculturalism or competence, but offers a different way to think about how we see, experience, and make an intentional investment in humanity through humility. Let us continue to explore the connection between relationships and humility that will lead to recovery when conflicts occur.

RELATIONSHIPS AND HUMILITY

In the previous chapter, the authors defined humility as freedom of arrogance, assumptions, and acidic commentary. Another perspective: humility is grace, recovery, restoration. It is also considered to be selfless, fragile, vulnerable, and even. All of these perspectives are a part of what makes the idea of humility challenging. Who wants to show their vulnerability and fragility? In many ways, our society does not support that notion as being a catalyst for strength and connection. Certainly, in the K–12 setting, humility, in the sense of vulnerability and fragility, might be viewed as a sign of weakness and an inability to manage your classroom.

However, one can build relationships that are not only meaningful but also honest and open in this way. These are virtues associated with being humble. It is the bedrock for cultural humility. It also draws upon one's ability to understand and to be understood, and build that understanding based on awareness, sensitivity, and responsiveness.

Simply put, the way in which you build authentic, genuine, and high-performance and engaged relationships is almost entirely on what you know to be true about a person and yourself. It is also how your behavior and actions respond to your knowledge and understanding. It is for these reasons that high-performance relationships are key to creating a culture and environment that can withstand climatic *shifts*. *Shifts* will be discussed in detail in chapter 7.

Let us revisit the Brookdale scenario to further example why this concept is important.

On this day, Mrs. Thomas sent Juan to the Principal's office with a disciplinary note. This has become a common occurrence over the last two weeks. Thirty minutes later, after being sent to the office, Juan is back. Mrs. Thomas is frustrated and upset that her administration does not appear to be supporting her. She angrily tells Juan to just sit in the corner. Juan complies and sneers at Mrs. Thomas. He's actually glad that Mrs. Thomas sent him to the corner. He needed the sleep anyway. His mind is on his brother and hoping that he is okay.

What is Mrs. Thomas failing to do that might help her understand Juan's behavior.

In this scenario, it might be an obvious response to insist that Juan tells Mrs. Thomas what is going on in his life. However, consider the lack of vulnerability, care, or sensitivity Mrs. Thomas has demonstrated. Why would Juan want to talk with Mrs. Thomas? What about her interactions and engagements, so far, with Juan demonstrated to him that he is in a brave or safe place, free from judgment and ridicule? This is not the makings of a high-performance or high-engagement relationship.

THE BENEFITS OF
HIGH-ENGAGEMENT RELATIONSHIPS

What happens when we bump into the darkness of bias? It can be argued that when one engages in biases, they perpetuate other-izing. In classrooms, those biases can be a major obstacle to the development of high-performance or authentic relationships between peers and between students and teachers.

In *High-Performance Relationships: The Heart and Science behind Success at Work and Home*, Dr. Jacqueline Peters suggests that high-performance relationships are a gateway of sorts to how individuals connect to each other and how people can create lasting authentic interactions. She presents five components to high-performance relationships: purpose, structure, camaraderie, and repair. These components, according to Peters, (2015), are based on our beliefs, values, and growth mindset. Does this sound familiar?

For the purposes of this discussion, the authors draw upon the work of Peters (2015) to identify the elements that promote conflict recovery, and ultimately, restoration. However, the focus here is about building and maintaining high-engagement relationships, not high-performance relationships, that are flexible, resilient, and authentic. These types of high-engagement relationships are not perfect or impermeable. These relationships can become central to recovery when a transgression or an assault is leveled against the relationship.

In Mrs. Thomas's case, she has a relationship with Juan, albeit a low-engagement relationship, that is ineffective and yielding negative results. Yet, with some considerable work, with Mrs. Thomas leading the way, both she and Juan can recover from the conflict or contentious situation that has led to a relationship break. It can start with cultural humility, lead to civility, and incorporate respect and personality at either end. But how? The next sections will take a deeper dive into the benefit of high-engagement relationships that can support conflict recovery.

COMPONENTS OF
HIGH-ENGAGEMENT RELATIONSHIPS

A high-engagement relationship is founded on three primary components: safety and belonging, accountability and investment, and recovery and restoration. Each component can strengthen or weaken the quality and amount of time individuals spend developing and maintaining this type of relationship, that when cultivated, yields mindfulness of support, openness, empathy, and a host of other valuable attributes.

SAFETY AND BELONGING

Safety and belonging are the bedrock and address two fundamental factors. One, when a person, or in this case, a student, is in a physically and psychologically safe environment, they are more likely to share, be vulnerable, and develop trust, and do so without the threat of retaliation or judgment. Many classroom teachers tout that they have safe spaces. However, saying you have a safe space and behaving or allowing behavior that reflects the opposite of safe is detrimental to the relationships one needs to build with students.

Safe and brave spaces can be very beneficial. These spaces allow students to share with people or with a person who is understanding and sensitive to their issue. It can be highly controlled areas where the student is free to be themselves. Whereas, a brave space might be a vulnerable space where individuals can share information which could change a mindset or influence someone's understanding and what they have always known to be true.

Two, safety and belonging speak to the level of trust, and the type of constructive conversation fostered and facilitated between the members of the classroom. The ability and commitment to developing trust strengthens the bonds between individuals in a healthy way. This can help those members engage in healthy conversations about their feelings, desires, fears, and so on. Trust can eventually help the teacher understand how to best support his or her students.

However, trust is also very fragile and requires a great deal of honesty and care to protect. It is not something which is easily given, and if broken, is very difficult to repair. It can also support the type of conversation a teacher may have with a student later—a conversation that, in many instances could be life-altering. This is why cultural humility—awareness, sensitivity, and responsiveness—is vital.

ACCOUNTABILITY AND INVESTMENT

One of the most important relationships you can have is the one you cultivate with yourself. Certainly, self-awareness is a perspective that describes a part of cultural humility. It is a process where one engages in discovery and self-renewal to open a pathway toward understanding others. When it comes to the idea of a high-engaged relationship, each member of the relationship is engaged in a type of interdependence, and each member is making a type of investment in the relationship. The investment may be large or small. The quality of the relationship may influence how each member understands the other person's commitment to the relationship—good or bad and the amount of time invested.

Accountability and investment also has a great deal to do with the type of agreements and relatedness purported. Meaning, what is it about the way in which you enter and exit a relationship that says, "I am present in the moment, and I am compelled to contribute to the relationship in a positive way." In some ways, it relates back to the level of trust between the parties involved. Additionally, in the K–12 classrooms, individuals enter and exit relationships with students consistently. The thinking, behavior, and actions will speak volumes to the value that is placed upon that relationship and how people choose to engage further.

RECOVERY AND RESTORATION

In chapter 1, the authors defined recovery as a return to a state of being. This definition is based upon the idea that the relationship and interactions were mostly positive and healthy, and there is a desire to return to that state. However, what happens when conflict alters the relationship? How do you manage a relationship that starts out rocky? What do you do when the road to recovery is long and arduous, or the personalities of the people involved in the conflict make it difficult to achieve a desired state of peace? What does one do in those instances? These questions guide recovery and restoration and are built on the general principles of restorative justice.

Without oversimplifying, restorative justice principle allows for the involved parties to reflect, investigate, discuss, attempt to make peace, and rebuild. This is critical to the overall concept of conflict recovery and the strategies that will be discussed later in this chapter. The principles of restorative justice can help one attempt to rebuild, return, or create something new. Therefore, to recover a broken relationship will require engagement in discussions where both parties negotiate reinvestment, safety, and opportunities for recovery.

It might also facilitate a reckoning of emotional wounds and hurt caused by the breakdown of the relationship. It is not an easy process, especially when the trust is bruised or broken. If one allows conflict to grow into a collision that can be fatal to the culture of the classroom and can be detrimental to the student and teacher, in this instance. It might also preclude opportunities to nourish the relationship. Therefore, any attempt to either reconcile, rebuild, and restore is better than the alternative.

CONFLICT RECOVERY

A quick review: conflict is a disagreement or quarrel. Recovery is described as a return to a state of being. *Conflict recovery* refers to the way one engages in cultural humility and civility to realign the relationship. It is how one's personality (values, beliefs, and qualities) breaks through a persona, (the way in which we represent or present ourselves to the world), to inspire authentic and genuine interactions.

Conflict recovery is an ongoing process of mindfulness and behavioral changes to avoid apathy, assumptions, arrogance, and the acidic commentary that only drives individuals further apart. It is using a process composed of various strategies to help guide how one might move toward those high-engagement relationships discussed earlier. The strategies presented in the next section should be used in a sequential way to achieve the most sustainable pathway toward connectedness and productivity that can withstand climatic change, especially within the classroom and between students and teachers.

Conflict recovery is based on the positive nature of the term "recover." It will be used as a mnemonic device to help the reader practice and apply the strategies with confidence. Figure 4 presents the seven strategies one might consider using to regain a healthy relationship, heal a broken relationship, or mediate between individuals in conflict. (See figure 4).

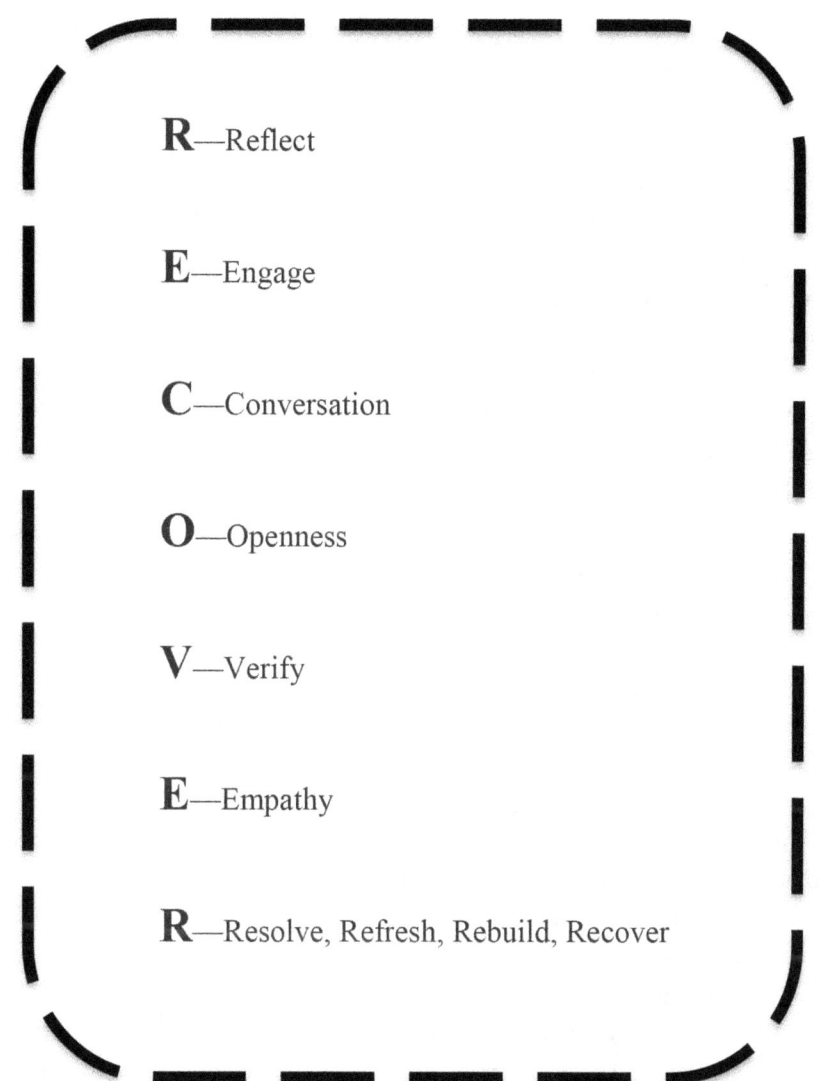

Figure 4

Reflect allows both parties to engage in some self-awareness and ask themselves questions about what they might not have considered. *Engage* is about taking the step to be vulnerable and ask for greater dialogue. This leads to the opportunity to come into an agreement, and perhaps, acknowledgment. As was mentioned earlier, the opportunity to simply engage in *conversation* can be powerful. However, depending on the type of conflict, a third party might help negotiate the conversation peacefully. This is a key principle of restorative justice.

Openness creates those opportunities for safe and brave spaces that allow for deeper understanding of self and others. Then you move into *verify* or investigation. This is a tricky step because you might be entering the conversation from an evidence or information gathering place. This is where some critical coaching questions might help facilitate the evidence gathering. In some ways to verify is also about trying to focus on what is happening at the moment and to confirm the points that caused a breakdown.

This is not the time to focus on blame or shame. It might be gathering information to investigate further and engage in some self-assessment. To verify might also mean that one is acknowledging the emotionality attached to the conflict, triggers, and the certain discomfort someone may have with discussing the conflict. Then one must promote *empathy* toward the situation, experience, and person or persons involved.

Empathy is generally categorized in three ways. Cognitive empathy is related to one's ability to think about how an experience may have affected someone else, even if you may not have a shared experience with that person. Emotional empathy is when someone connects with another person's experience. They have the same or a similar type of experience. Then there is compassionate empathy, which is where most people believe they are, but compassionate empathy is typically achieved when one engages in an action to help resolve the conflict, in this instance.

Finally, one can progress toward *resolve*, rebuilding, and recovery. This might mean that the parties have come into agreement. It might mean they have a better understanding of the conflict or circumstances that lead to the conflict. They might create steps they will use to avoid further conflict and attempt to rebuild the relationship, especially if the relationship was broken.

Let us revisit Mrs. Thomas's and Juan's story to determine how R-E-C-O-V-E-R might be used effectively.

After several more days of contentious interactions, Mrs. Thomas asks her Principal for help. Besides the behavioral issues, she is now becoming concerned about Juan missing several days a week at school. When she asked Juan about it, his answers are usually vague and dismissive. She is keenly aware that this cannot continue, and she wants to find a way to help Juan.

FINAL THOUGHTS

The final section of this chapter provides some questions to help you reflect upon the information and how it might be applied to the scenario and personal experiences. There is also an activity—*script, share, work*—designed to help you add contexture to your understanding of conflict recovery. As you work though the questions and activity, think about how you might use the activity in your work setting to help others realize the importance of conflict recovery.

The next chapter will focus on the leader. Specifically, chapter 7 will discuss the culture and ethos that a leader creates and how to handle the SHIFTS that will occur frequently. Chapter 7 will also revisit Brookdale High from the leader's perspective.

Script-Share-Work Activity

The script-share-work activity is an opportunity to create a dialogue that one could use for future purposes when faced with, in this case, a conflict. This activity guides you through three steps. First, you think about a time or situation in which your response (behavior or action) might have been different. Then, either you share those experiences, in a small group, with a thought partner, or you might reflect on the script yourself. Finally, the work involves referencing this new information in the future. Use the following example activity to model how you might use this type of activity in the future.

Instructions: Think back to a time or an experience in which you committed a misdeed or mishandled a situation—a time when your response was not effective or perhaps offensive. Maybe it was a neglected deadline that caused a domino effect. Perhaps it was a lying to an authority figure to avoid persecution. Maybe it was participating in spreading negative information about someone else. Maybe a hostile response to a student, colleague, or parent caused a break in an otherwise productive relationship.

Use this experience as the foundation to have a conversation between your current self and your past self from this experience. Keep this question in mind as you work through the next steps, "What advice would I give my current self to resolve this internal struggle?" (Author emphasis)

Script

Begin your script as your current self, speaking to your past self by utilizing the RECOVER strategy (figure 4) earlier in the chapter. Act as if your current self is trying to educate your past self on how to carefully, but genuinely engage in the recovery strategy. Remember, you will be scripting for your current self, as well as replying as your past self. Here is starter example.

Current Self:

"Hey John. You remember when you didn't turn in that paperwork on time? It put the whole team behind the 8 ball." Reflect and engage.

Past Self:

"Yeah, I know John. But it's not like the team was really hurt by me missing the deadline. If so, they never said anything to me about it. Engage and conversation."

Current Self: "They may not have said anything, but their body language said a lot. Besides, this was a critical part of the project and your procrastination caused a lot of unnecessary stress. I don't need to let my issues affect the team. Let me get this done!"

Openness, Verify, Empathy, and Resolve.

Using your experience, write a script with as much as dialogue as necessary as you initiate the RECOVER strategy with the example. One way to work through a productive script is to overlap key areas to add to the richness of the dialogue.

Share

After the dialogue is complete, use a recording device of your convenience to recite the conversation, either video or audio. Be sure to insert the proper inflections of the conversation for optimal effect. Again, you are attempting to convince your past self that there is a method of providing recovery for situations of conflict.

Work

Once you have completed the recording, play it for someone else, or at least for yourself. See if you or others can recognize at which stages of the

RECOVER strategy are you most confident. Also, at which stages would you require more coaching. With more practice, the strategy can become more organic in use. Try scripting another incident from your past experiences to become more adept at the RECOVER strategy.

THINK, REFLECT, CONNECT

1) Have you experienced a similar type of situation? How might this information have helped you engage in conflict recovery? What could Mrs. Thomas do at this point?
2) Why is high-engagement relationship beneficial in the classroom? How does not having those types of relationships influence the culture and climate?

_____
_____
_____
_____
_____

REFERENCE

Peters, J (2015). *High performance relationships: The heart and science behind success at work and home.* InnerActive Leadership Associates.

Chapter 7

Leading

Understanding the Cultural SHIFTS

"The first function of education is to provide identity."

—*Dr. Na'im Akbar*

It's Wednesday afternoon and Dr. Dillinger desperately wants to take a break from the constant interruptions, disagreements between her staff, and challenges teachers are facing with the students. Her school sits in the middle of a neighborhood that has changed drastically and many of the teachers have a very difficult time understanding some of the challenges these families face on a day-to-day basis. Some of the teachers hold values and beliefs that are completely opposite of their student demographics and sometimes that causes even more problems.

Her most recent conversation with Mrs. Thomas about one her students, Juan, was similar to many conversations she's had with teachers over the last two weeks. If only they could take a moment to try and learn who their students really are outside of the classroom. She knows it would help them figure out what to do in the classroom and how to offer genuine support for them—or, at the very least, be open to understanding.

One thing she knows for sure is that she has to figure out a way to shift the culture in the school to withstand some of the climate changes that will continue to affect the students. Her students are worried about their families, school, and a host of other things. Teachers seem apathetic. This cannot go on for the good of the school. Her thoughts begin to drift to a leadership coaching session on culture management she attended over the summer.

One of the primary responsibilities of the school leader is to establish the school's ethos—the way in which the cultural spirit is manifested through values and beliefs of the people who, in this case, live, learn, and develop in school. This school's ethos is driven by a desire to succeed and a need to meet standards and outcomes at a high level. What is often the most challenging aspect of a school's ethos is managing the relationships between the members of the ethos. Moreover, it is the recognition that the *SHIFTS* can greatly impact how the ethos withstands climatic changes which will occur, and can occur often, and how one interacts and build relationships with one another in the school.

This chapter will explore the *SHIFTS*—an acronym that reflects a framework to help leaders focus on acknowledging principles and considerations that will allow for relationships to develop through the practice of cultural humility and civility. Toward the end of the chapter, there will be an activity to help you facilitate deep discussion about your current and desired ethos.

Additionally, a visual is presented to foster conceptualizing how one navigates conflict and compromise and moves toward more constructive approaches. The chapter will also encourage leaders to reflect on how restorative justice principles can be used with staff and students. Finally, the chapter will revisit Dr. Dillinger periodically to example how one might consider using these concepts effectively. Let us first start with an exploration of ethos and an understanding of *SHIFTS*.

THE IMPORTANCE OF ETHOS

Oftentimes when someone says the word "culture," one might naturally think of race, ethnicity, and such. However, culture for this discussion refers to the school culture, which fosters a sense of learning, accountability, and for the purposes of this book, humility and civility. Establishing a culture is no easy task and requires the leader to consider the way in which the ethos dictates how the culture moves and feels to its members.

To build and manage a healthy school culture, not only does the leader need to pay attention to the climatic shifts that can affect the overall culture, the leader should also focus on other key objectives to ensure all members within the culture have a stake in ensuring the culture is healthy. Those objectives include:

- Keeping a finger on the pulse of the culture. Talk to staff and students. Know what is going on in the community, students' families, if necessary. Check in with staff informally and formally.
- Identify the positive aspects of your culture that you want to enhance and be honest about the areas that need improving. Bring in key partners to help make the necessary improvements.
- Establish community principles and norms to set boundaries and expectations within the school and classroom. These principles should be affirming statements and express positive thoughts.
- Develop a reasonable behavior guidance plan which should be based on cultural humility and civility and tout conflict recovery as an alternative to suspension.
- Provide teachers with ongoing opportunities for professional development on humility, equity, and inclusion until those conversations are normalized.
- Engage in consistent and ongoing fidelity checks to measure successes and opportunities for improvement.

The origin of ethos is based on the idea of customs, dispositions, habits, and the character of a time and place. These are some of the elements leaders should focus on in the ethos. Certainly, a school culture has customs, habits of being and characteristics; however, what makes ethos a bit different is that it also speaks to the spirit of that time and place. This is significant as it reflects the sensitivity to self and others—an element of cultural humility. It is the acknowledgement that a school's culture has an ethos that creates an energy that students and staff can embrace, support, and promote.

There are four components of an ethos—empathy, active listening, healthy conversations, and humility. Each component plays a significant role in the way a culture responds to the members and how each member response in it. Together these components serve as a platform on which conflict recovery and restorative practices can successfully help manage and maintain a healthy culture. Let us explore each component in more detail.

EMPATHY IN THE ETHOS

There are three generally accepted types of empathy. Cognitive empathy addresses how we think about others and their feelings. It is a type of basic understanding—an awareness. Emotional empathy refers to how one makes a personal connection to another person's narrative, story, and circumstance. They may have a shared experience that allows for a deeper understanding of how that situation is affecting the person's behavior or thinking.

The last type of empathy is compassionate empathy. Arguably, most people believe they are engaged in compassionate empathy when, in fact, they are not. Compassionate empathy means that one is taking action based upon the value placed on what they know, and how they connect to what they know. Compassionate empathy is probably the most difficult to achieve because one cannot sit on the sidelines. You are compelled to advocate, act, think deeply, or engage others in an action toward a greater good.

In an educational setting, it is quite possible that empathy drives a critical piece of an ethos. Students and staff are experiencing, thinking, and engaging on multiple levels and in various ways. Attempting to understand a person's feelings is essential to creating an environment that demonstrates care and thoughtfulness. A positive ethos where people are sensitive to each other's behavior and thinking speaks to the essence of compassionate empathy. Moreover, as you learn more about an individual's story, it is quite possible that you will find areas where one might connect across racial and cultural barriers. This is important to guide a group toward achieving the care and compassionate empathy that allows a school to thrive.

ACTIVE LISTENING IN THE ETHOS

Being present in the moment is key to active listening. When one is engaged in active listening, they are listening to understand and not listening to respond. Listening to understand means one is exercising an element of cultural humility—awareness, because awareness means that you are building knowledge, adding to your knowledge, or correcting your understanding. It is the deepening of awareness that directly affects thinking.

Active listening is not engaging in a casual conversation. It is an effort to free oneself from distractions that signals to the person with whom you are speaking, that what they are saying is important and valued. This type of valuing also helps the parties to build trust in one another and one's body language might indicate there are no judgements being made. In essence, it supports the definition of civility the authors of this book describes as "respect and valuing the humanity."

Imagine how critical active listening is to building an ethos—the cultural spirit of the school that says everyone is respected and valued, and their backgrounds, and histories will not be weaponized against them. The functionality of active listening is hugely important to the way in which people respond to one another and is directly connected to the overall concept of conflict recovery. If one is present in the moment and listening to understand, they might learn something new. They may use this new concept or construct to provide clarity when difficult conversations occur.

HEALTHY CONVERSATIONS IN THE ETHOS

There is a 100 percent chance that a difficult conversation will happen in a school. The questions are as follows: (1) How do you handle it and how do you respond? (2) What will your behavior indicate about your thinking? (3) What type of strategy or process will you have to manage a conflict or challenging conversation? Later in this chapter, the authors will present a visual to help leaders and others negotiate conflict and compromise using the *Civility Control Scale*. The scale provides a visual reminder of a continuum to reach consensus and steer away from collisions.

A strategy that might be helpful to leaders, especially when entering and existing difficult conversations is the PRPLE sandwich. It is a communication strategy presented in *Success Favors Well-Prepared teachers: Relationships and Routines for Improved School Culture*. The strategy suggests that one enters the conversations with a positive affirmation, then a statement of fact or evidence—the reality.

Then, offer a statement that signifies the potential for change or understanding that might include a time in which the person exhibited a desired result or disposition. The next technique is an accountability statement (leverage) and ends with motivating statement to empower the person to act. Each technique might be used in various stages of the conversation, but one should always start with an affirmation and end with motivation.

Chapter 7

HUMILITY IN THE ETHOS

The final element in an ethos is humility. In the previous chapter, the authors defined and described humility. It is the foundation of the entire book and is woven throughout every aspect of conflict recovery. Humility allows one to acknowledge that the other person is the narrator of his or her own story. Their story should be honored and accepted as that person's truth. This is critical even when one might be in disagreement or when they have differing values and beliefs.

Humility can be particularly helpful during those times when closure is not the desired effect, but understanding and acknowledgement is what truly matters. Together, empathy, active listening, difficult conversation strategies, and humility create a culture—an ethos where recovery and restoration is the status quo. In order for the leader to promote and attend to these critical elements of an ethos, the leader must also pay attention to how the shifts, which will be discussed next, affects the culture's personality and persona. Before that, let us check in on Dr. Dillinger and the ethos within Brookdale.

Brookdale is experiencing some significant challenges. Dr. Dillinger decided to meet with her leadership coach to talk about what she could do and how to change the tide of discontent in the school. She is increasingly becoming frustrated with her teachers and know her students are experiencing traumas that many of her teachers have never experienced, but who also have not discussed in their classrooms.

Her leadership coach, acting as a thinking partner and sounding board, walked her through a series of questions to help her come to some conclusions and next steps. The first place was to start with a conversation about the school's culture and how she, Dr. Dillinger, might make some changes they moved through the questions, Dr. Dillinger quickly realized she needed to make have some difficult conversations with key people and she needed to implement some more substantive approaches that would rebuild trust and safety in her school. (Author emphasis)

Based on what you know so far about Brookdale, where might Dr. Dillinger need to focus her attention to make improvements with the school's culture beyond engaging in some difficult conversations? Later in the chapter, you will have an opportunity to think about your school's ethos.

EXPLORING THE SHIFTS

SHIFTS is an acronym for sight, hearing, intuition, freedom, taste, and smell. It focuses on three major themes in a school's culture, the sights and sounds, freedom and flexibility, and soul and spirit (Parker & Barnes, 2018). Those overarching themes will be discussed, in brief, later in the chapter. Typically, school culture is a complex system of people, policies, politics, and promises where compliance is king, and the culture is often dictated by a desire for achievement and success. However, if the *shifts* are not attended to, a school's culture can become quite toxic and the ethos breathes negativity.

Imagine how empathy, active listening, conversations, and humility can be debunked in a toxic culture. It becomes a school where people exist, collect paychecks, and little to no accountability for learning happens. Furthermore, in schools challenged by various external and internal struggles, the more desired effects take a backseat and the ethos—the cultural spirit fails to thrive. This is a prime reason why paying attention to *shifts* with the ethos is important. It is an ongoing process of paying attention to the climatic patterns, in and out of the school, as in the case of Brookdale High that will further define the school's culture as healthy and thriving.

When approaching the concept of *shifts*, these three outcomes are integrated into the idea. The leader must pay attention to the sights and sounds within the culture first. This means looking beyond the optics and addressing the reality that make the optics real and substantive. Dressing up the culture is akin to putting a bandage over a festering wound. You want the sights and sounds to be in response to the way in which the members build relationships, engage in conversations, and offer grace and recovery when necessary. When that occurs, what one sees in the culture, and what one hears in the culture, reflects reality.

Second, intuition helps to form the freedom and flexibility within the culture. In some ways, intuition reflects how we value and respect the humanity of each member within the school's culture. Intuition works to ensure that the culture does not support judgement and mistrust that will surely affect the culture and its members negatively. As members grow and discover more about themselves and others, it can make it easier to implement conflict recovery. It might even motivate individuals to take risks academically, as well as, socio-emotionally, trusting that their narrative will be honored.

Parallel to feelings and flexibilities of a culture are the interactions between the adults. The social barriers, and sometimes, the bias boundaries, that one ascribes to occlude adult interactions. These barriers can sanitize an individual's ability to acknowledge other people's values and beliefs. By not encouraging this element of freedom, (acknowledging others values and beliefs and allowing them to do the same for you), it can further interrupt the pathways toward trust. The leader is then tasked to be vigilant in cultivating the ethos to allow for judgement free zones and encourage the members to practice strategies saturated with humility and civility.

Finally, the soul and spirit draws upon all three elements of cultural humility—awareness, responsiveness, and sensitivity—to address how the culture intersects with emotionality. However, the soul and spirit is not something one can readily see, but there might be indications of how a school's culture makes someone feel given the sights and sounds. For example, Mrs. Thomas, Dr. Dillinger, and Juan all have feelings about Brookdale High. These feelings are displayed in a variety of ways in and out of the classroom. Those feelings, therefore, are reflected in their conversations, their body language, their interactions, their relationships, and their engagement. It is the soul and spirit within a culture that floods the senses and makes the members react positively or negatively.

In general, *shifts* attempts to respond to what the culture looks like, sounds like, feels like, and acts like. A leader must always question:

- Is it a culture that reflects of healing or a culture of hurt and harm?
- Is it a culture where civility is dressed up as polite gesturing?
- Is it a culture where the members rely on a collective identity, a supportive energy, principles, and practices that guide positive interactions and relationships?
- Is it a culture where cultural humility is king and conflict recovery is a mechanism to right a ship?

Paying attention to the *shifts* is a full-time job. A leader must be able to answer these questions and build a sense of confidence in his or her ability to explore the school's culture and implement strategies and supplant others when necessary to speak to the members' needs, talents, challenges, and opportunities for success. Establishing a culture that can withstand climatic change will benefit everyone involved because the members will have an ethos of great care, consideration, and compassion.

Here are a few considerations to simulate further thoughts about acknowledging and utilizing the *S.H.I.F.T.S.* when establishing and cultivating a school culture and an activity that you can use to engage your team in a discussion about your school's culture and ethos.

- Attending to sights and sounds without substance is not sustainable.
- Focus on cultivating relationships and practices that will guide the culture.
- Create a space that demonstrates through thinking, actions, and behaviors that feelings, emotions, thoughts, and ideas will be honored.
- Energize your members to help you co-construct the culture they want to live and learn in.
- Show your vulnerability. It reflects your humanity.

There are three outcomes the leader should expect to achieve that will reflect the strength and resiliency of the school's culture. Some of the objectives discussed previously are baked into these outcomes.

- Relationships where cultural humility and civility are at the foundation. As the leader, it is important to model genuineness and intentionality to get to know students and staff. A critical part of that is practicing strategies to resolve conflict. When students witness staff engaging in strategies to collaborate or manage conflict, it offers students some explicit examples to influence their capabilities.
- Effective restorative justice, recovery, and conflict management strategies and plans. This can provide opportunities for students to have a voice and choice in the development of the policies, procedures, and practices. It also speaks volumes to the implementation of productive and instructive strategies to address conflicts and difficult conversations. Remember that a principle of conflict recovery is conversation and openness. Using a visual reminder, such as the *Civility Control Scale*, with staff, and perhaps students, can be helpful to the recovery implementation process.

The *Civility Control Scale*, pictured, helps one focus on the potential for engagements and interactions to be positive or negative depending on the person's personality and substance or topic of the discussion. It can also help one determine the point where the conversation or interaction moved in an undesired direction toward collision and confrontation. (See figure 5).

Figure 5 Civility Control Scale.

However, it is important to note that confrontation, while viewed unfavorable, is about truth. Certainly, most people welcome a conversation in truth as opposed to a conversation in falsity. Conversely, most individuals welcome collaboration where the group is united. The authors suggest that while collaboration is achievable, it takes a great deal of cultivation. The leader should also acknowledge that consensus still has the propensity to move a culture in a positive direction, should that be where the group lands before reaching full collaboration.

- A school climate of making informed decisions on empirical, anecdotal, and formative data. This might mean that the members of the culture are engaging in assimilation or acculturation. Depending on the personality of the leader, assimilation and acculturation can guide members to either convert to a current ethos or adopt different beliefs and values that could change the ethos to be more inclusive of its members. In either case, each member will make a commitment through his or her actions, activities, and experiences to attend to the shifts, and do so, by focusing on relationships and data-informed strategic planning.

The *Building Ethos* is an activity to help one shape a path toward awareness and action. It is designed for individuals and teams to engage in discussions about the values and beliefs currently held in the culture. It is also designed to engage the user in thinking about a desired ethos and who the actors and players are to make that ethos a realization, and how the group will measure success. It can also be used as a brainstorming tool to begin creating what conflict recovery will look like, sounds like, and feel like in the school. Below is a tool to help you get started. (See figure 6).

Building Ethos				
Describe your current Ethos. What are the beliefs, values, and characteristics of the cultural that speaks to how the culture feels, looks, and sounds?	What are the processes, understandings, and values that support the current ethos?	What would your ideal ethos LOOK like, SOUND like, and FEEL like?	Who, or what would you need to make the desired/ideal ethos a reality (i.e., resources.)?	What are the benchmarks to help you measure your successes? What are the steps you can implement?

Figure 6 Building Ethos Tool.

Let us revisit Brookdale to see how Dr. Dillinger is faring.

After careful consideration and multiple conversations with key staff and students, Dr. Dillinger decided to create some type of restorative justice team. She has asked Mrs. Johnson, the counselor, to take the lead on the effort. First, though, she reworked the professional development schedule and the professional learning communities to walk each team through the ethos activity. She was really interested in learning from her staff if there was a culture that supported the ethos and an ethos that reflected the culture.

She also engaged staff members in coaching conversations designed to help the teachers acknowledge and critique their own understanding about who their students are and the various experiences in the community that are affecting their students. She was pleased with some of her staff's progress and desire to see the school function differently. It was evident to many teachers especially that they have been holding students to unrealistic goals without really understanding the challenges these students face.

Mrs. Thomas, while at first was defensive, as she perceived herself culturally competent, quickly realized that she really did not understand Juan's story. The story she told herself about him was not wholly accurate and riddled with assumptions. After taking the time to show some vulnerability and accountability for her thinking, which started with her simply apologizing to Juan for making up his story—a story that only made sense to her. By doing this, she opened the door for more conversation that allowed her to see Juan differently while still holding him responsible for his learning and behavior. She learned that Juan's brother was deported. This then made it necessary for Juan to find a job to help support his family. And his acting out in class was a product of frustration and exhaustion. This was eye opening. She is hoping that Juan will agree to be a part of the team Dr. Dillinger is creating.

FINAL THOUGHTS

Ethos and culture are intertwined. The four elements of an ethos can support the overall school culture. A school's culture can be defined by its ethos. While, yes, it is the leader's responsibility to facilitate, prime, and shape the culture—the ethos, the various other members of the culture will project the values and beliefs of the ethos into the culture. What does your school's culture and ethos say about how you lead and how you would like to lead?

More importantly, how do you as the leader model the behaviors and actions that you would want to see, and implement strategies that foster deep cultural humility and civility? The next section poses additional questions for consideration, and in the next chapter, you will revisit Brookdale from the school-based mental health perspective.

THINK, REFLECT, CONNECT

1) Think about a time when your story about a student or colleague was vastly different from their reality. How did your thinking or behavior change? Did you engage in a conversation that moved your future engagements to a more positive position?
2) How might the *Civility Control Scale* have helped you visualize the pathway in one direction or the other? If the engagement endpoint was negative, can you identify the point at which that happened, and can you identify the steps you took to move toward a more positive position?
3) What are the beliefs and values that drive your ethos, and how could this information be used to affect change in your educational setting?
4) Which one of the *shifts* is helpful to, or challenging in, your school, and why?

_____
_____
_____
_____
_____

REFERENCES

Parker, T. S. & Barnes, C. D. (2018). Remember the S.H.I.F.T.S to establish an effective school culture. *The Journal of Effective Schools Project*, 25(1).

Parker, T. S., Barnes, C. D., & Kohler-Evans, P. (2016). *Success favors well-prepared teachers: Developing routines and relationships to improve school culture.* Lanham, MD: Rowman & Littlefield, Publishers.

Chapter 8

Counseling

Cultural Humility for the Mental Health Professional in Schools

"People of different religions and cultures live side by side in almost every part of the world, and most of us have overlapping identities which unite us with very different groups. We can love what we are, without hating what – and who – we are not. We can thrive in our own tradition, even as we learn from others, and come to respect their teachings."

—*Kofi Annan, Former Secretary-General of the United Nations*

Returning to Brookdale High from the previous chapters. The school is majority-minority. Many of the students' families are immigrants from Africa and Central American countries. Some family members are undocumented. The majority of the staff are white, young women from middle-class backgrounds. Most teachers and other personnel teach at Brookdale between 2–4 years on average and leave for "better" schools in the suburbs.

The last several weeks at Brookdale has been uniquely challenging because of the clash between students and teachers, which is heightened by a recent ICE raid that took several students' parents and close family members away. This only made the trust issues worse, and some of the students believe that many of the teachers played a role in the raids. Mrs. Johnson, the school counselor, started her career at Brookdale twelve years ago and has seen it change dramatically over those years. She understands the students' concerns and is one of the few people whom students confide in and talk to on a regular basis.

After talking with a few students, teachers, and Mrs. Thomas, the Principal, she thought it might be a good idea to be proactive and try and stem the tide of the racial tension by applying restorative justice principles. One thing she knows for sure is the students and the teachers have strained relationships. Given the issues in the community will not likely change, the teachers need to have a better understanding of how all of this will affect their classrooms and the overall school.

Mrs. Johnson started by obtaining approval from Mrs. Thomas to develop a restorative justice team; she aptly named Brookdale Nations, a play on the United Nations, given the multiple countries represented in the school. She then worked with the administration to select teachers to be a part of Brookdale Nations. She and the administration were strategic in selecting teachers from diverse backgrounds, who would also promote the idea and be a positive and productive influence to ensure the idea had good and solid footing.

Once the teachers were selected and provided some preliminary information on what this group would do and how it would work to mend or repair relationships, she asked them to select some students to join the team; however, they were asked to not just pick students who were compliant and received A's. They were asked to pick students who would be honest, open to providing feedback, and who represented a variety of cultural backgrounds.

Later on, in this chapter, we will examine their first meeting as a group, but first, think about these questions:

1. What do you think Mrs. Johnson plans to do with this group? Why is it important that the group be representative?
2. Do you have similar issues at your own school? How do you think a group like this would go over? Would there be administration push back?

In the previous chapters, the authors shared the origin and background of cultural humility. The concept is emerging as a gold standard for working with clients of diverse backgrounds and identities within a therapeutic setting. The overall nature of cultural humility challenges the idea of competence and allows one to accept a different frame of thinking about self and others.

The implications of cultural humility and civility and a more in-depth description of conflict recovery were presented. An insightful look into the leader's role in creating an ethos that supports cultural humility and civility by attending to the SHIFTS was also discussed in the previous chapters; however, this chapter seeks to focus on cultural humility and civility from a mental health standpoint.

This chapter will further the discussion to focus on the shift from competence from a mental health perspective to the implementation of restorative justice principles within the school. The role of the mental health professional to promote cultural humility and civility as the foundation will be key to this discussion. Throughout the chapter, the reader will revisit Brookdale High to reflect on how mental health professionals can be integral to ensuring a process or a system is incorporated into the culture of the school designed to create awareness, sensitivity, responsiveness, and ultimately, recovery, and restoration. First, a brief discussion on the dangers of a competence mind-set from a mental health perspective, especially in schools where young minds are terribly impressionable.

THE DANGERS OF THE COMPETENCE MIND-SET

Cultural competence could be causing more damage and limit professionals by reinforcing stereotypes and ignoring differences that speaks to a person's lived and loved experiences. If you accept the idea that diversity is a science that moves from the sociocultural construct to a psychological phenomenon that cannot be dismissed as a choice, then the way in which we understand the necessity to be inclusive and practice equity changes. This is critical to shift from competence to humility—where one cannot assume, they are competent in something as fluid as a culture. Moreover, one cannot generalize one experience to an entire group. It is easy for this competent mind-set to be a by-product of privilege.

Privilege is often unseen when you are the holder of it. This is a cautionary statement about how privilege could affect that work, despite efforts to the contrary. Furthermore, when one sees themselves as having high cultural competence, those individuals are less likely to be culturally competent because they see culture as an endpoint and not circular and evolving.

These findings have led some researchers to suspect that the traditional "competence" framework might actually be perpetuating stereotypes and leading to more confidence in the "I'm right because I'm competent" mindset. When people are treated as though they are members of a cultural group, their individual identities, all the different intersections, and their different life experiences are being dismissed and possibly dismantled for a more comfortable narrative as we see with Mrs. Thomas.

Cultural humility, however, is a process of growth that operates under "the more I know about this person and their culture, the more I realize I don't know this person or their culture." Through continual self-awareness and critical self-reflection, a person chases after competence while realizing that they will never actually achieve competence.

There is also the issue that individuals tend to overestimate their competence when it comes to working with people who are of a different background. No one wants to think or believe they are incompetent, and so, their true competence is hyperinflated. This is distinctly true when the topic of race is dropped into the conversation, which can be quite problematic for counselors.

Mental health professionals rely heavily on relationships in order to provide adequate services to their clients. In fact, in therapy, it is widely accepted that the relationship between a client and a therapist accounts for 30 percent of the variance in therapeutic outcomes (Lambert & Barley, 2001). Therefore, if a counselor believes him or herself to be competent, they might miss an opportunity to understand their client on a deeper level and could potentially damage the relationship. In schools, almost every encounter with students is limited except for some of the more complex cases, and therefore, the relationships counselors have with students can influence the quantity and quality of the services provided.

Regardless of the technique or therapeutic orientation, understanding a person's culture and how they identify is a huge factor in forming a relationship with them. So, the questions become as follows:

1) How do mental health professionals and counselors develop trusting relationships with students and others, especially when there may be stark or significant cultural or racial differences?
2) How might one overestimate their competence when working with individuals who are different, and how might that overestimation hinder the relationships and services provided?

The answer to both questions is to build a system—a process for conflict recovery grounded in humility, specifically cultural humility, conflict recovery, and social and restorative justice principles. For the mental health professional, there also must be consideration of how to provide trauma-informed care for students who come from diverse backgrounds and who might be challenged by societal and structural issues.

TRAUMA-INFORMED CARE FOR CULTURALLY AND RACIALLY DIVERSE STUDENTS

Mental health and counseling approaches were primarily based on the culture and background of white, middle-class standards. The way in which questions are designed, methods implemented, and services provided was based on very narrow demographics whose experience differs greatly from, for example, a single, impoverished mother living in a neighborhood overrun with crime.

Therefore, if one uses the same techniques for both, then one group of clients may not receive appropriate services, simply because their experiences and needs are different. How, then, might these approaches be transferred to young people—students who come from affluence versus students who come from poverty. The neighborhood, circumstances, experiences, access to quality food, housing, and resources might be drastically different. Therefore, the needs of each individual student are different. That is not to equate students of color with poverty; however, there are disproportionately minority students who attended poorly resourced schools.

This phenomenon has been highlighted over the past few years with a movement encouraging more individuals of color to seek mental health services and the questions surrounding the post-traumatic stress of those living in high-poverty, low-access communities where some of the most tragic conditions are almost normalized. When those students enter school, those experiences come with them.

Students might be exposed to violence, feel unsafe in their homes, or have experienced negative encounters with law enforcement. They see people who look like them killed for seemingly doing nothing more than walking down a street in the media. This trauma can have an extremely negative effect on them.

Now imagine this student is in a classroom where all of these experiences, his identity, his way of being is misunderstood and in a school where his survival mechanisms, as bad behavior, or his calls for help are dismissed by his teacher and other school personnel. The standard ways of treating these students may not work if the counselor is unwilling to see that student's humanity and invest in cultural humility—awareness, sensitivity, and responsiveness. Let us see how Mrs. Johnson is using this information with her Brookdale Nations team.

After Brookdale Nations was finally constructed, Mrs. Johnson worked with the team to develop some community principles to determine how the group would work together. It was important that each person on the team, student and teacher, consider themselves to be equal partners in the process. This was no easy task, as both the teachers and students saw the teacher as the authority figure. However, once the students, in particular, realized the teachers wanted to co-construct the principles and held themselves accountable to the principles; it opened the door for some trust to grow. This was just a first step with many more to come to ensure this would work. Her next step was to engage the group on some activity to facilitate a deeper awareness of self and each person on the team. (Author emphasis)

RESTORATIVE JUSTICE

Recent research suggests that trauma is to blame for the rise of behavior problems and disabilities in the school (National Child Traumatic Stress Network, 2017). Trauma can come from a variety of sources and can actually affect the brain development of children, which can have lifelong consequences. Because of these findings, there is more and more discussion of trauma-informed curriculum and assessment.

According to the National Child Traumatic Stress Network (2017), trauma comes in a variety of forms: (1) experiencing or witnessing serious injury or death, (2) facing imminent threats of serious injury or death, or (3) experiencing a violation of personal or physical integrity. There is also the concept of historical trauma, which is the cumulative emotional and psychological trauma that can be transmitted across generations (National Child Traumatic Stress Network, 2017). This is often the case for racial and ethnic groups that have suffered intergenerational challenges. One major form of trauma seen in the schools today is racial trauma, which comes as a result of witnessing or experiencing racism, discrimination, or institutional racism. This form of trauma largely affects many schools today, whether it is done knowingly or unknowingly (National Child Traumatic Stress Network, 2017).

We still see the youth of color disproportionately represented in special education and office discipline referrals, despite the conversations that have been had about addressing the achievement gap. Students in the school system are exposed to racism through the media, experience, and history, and they need help navigating how to cope with this. That is why restorative justice principles are a necessary component of any educational system.

Restorative justice principles help to hold students accountable while also promoting positive relationships. The goal is for students to resolve conflicts on their own. It is a way to build empathy in students, which is something that is sorely lacking in this day and age. It also helps them to problem-solve additional ways of dealing with adverse situations.

RESTORATIVE JUSTICE AND CULTURAL HUMILITY

Restorative justice is centered on relationships and having trust and respect, and openness. Does this sound familiar? It should! Cultural humility is a lifestyle change that goes hand in hand with restorative justice. School mental health professionals understand that every individual has attributes, beliefs, experiences, and so on that shapes their personality and creates their persona. Cultural humility and restorative justice employs the notion that one must respect that individual and their identities and teach others to respect one another. One way to promote restorative justice is to be proactive about teaching cultural humility.

Teaching students and others to value one another—their backgrounds, histories, and values—is a huge part of restorative justice. It does not mean that you replace your values or transpose your values to them. It means that you acknowledge who they are, how they live, and the experiences that shape their lives. This perspective-taking allows students and adults to empathize with one another and to respect one another. It is the job of mental health professionals to promote the valuing of self and others, and one way to do that is by practicing and implanting cultural humility into the culture—the ethos of the school.

This next section presents a plan to help start the implementation of these principles from a school-based mental health approach. This is by no means a one-size-fits-all approach. However, this implementation plan can be used to generate thoughts, ideas, and activities for your school.

IMPLEMENTATION OF CONFLICT RECOVERY AND PEACE CIRCLES

Anyone who has ever tried to implement anything new in a school system knows that it is not an overnight process. It has to be integrated throughout the school, and this can only be done in small steps that move toward a larger goal. Each step of the process requires everyone being on the same page, actively engaged in training, using data to inform decisions, and so on. The best approach is to start small to promote better implementation and buy-in. Once there is data, then it is easier to approach other key personnel to roll it out school-wide.

There are several approaches that have been outlined by Mindy Willard (2018) that are easy to implement, especially within a mental health context. One example is a *proactive circle/ talking circle*. These circles allow adults and children to build trust and respect and help repair harm. Each person in the skill building should be allowed to talk, but only when they have the talking piece. This gives everyone the chance to be seen and heard. Another option is to have a *restorative circle*, which is focused on repairing broken relationships. In this circle, it is essential to ask questions such as the following:

1. What happened?
2. How have you felt since?
3. Who has been affected, and in what way?
4. What do you think needs to happen to restore the relationship?

The power is given to the students, in this instance, to explore, problem-solve, and heal the damage that has been done. Making these circles a common occurrence when issues arise is one way to start the implementation process. These circles can be effective tools for conflict recovery.

The circles can take place in a counselor's office, in small group sessions, or in response to office discipline referrals. It might also be that the circles are used to negotiate broken relationships between students, colleagues, or even the student-teacher relationship. One could then collect data periodically as a part of the fidelity checking mechanism to determine what is working and what needs improvement and the implementation moves forward.

Another idea for the implementation of conflict recovery is to use a Response to Intervention (RTI) approach. The first tier of this would be a school-wide implementation of the language and the belief system. Use of proactive circles regularly can help achieve that step. The second tier would be more intensive and devoted to those who need more skills and intervention. For example, when two students get into a fight or if punitive action would normally be taken for a behavior, perhaps a recovery circle might be used instead.

Finally, tier three should be only a few students who need intensive supervision. In this tier, students who have been removed or are under consideration for a move from the regular education classroom would receive intervention that is most intensive. This tier is designed to help them learn about restorative principles and other social skills that are needed for reintegration.

Let us peek into how Mrs. Johnson has used the information to implement a plan for conflict recovery and restoration. The implementation plan includes links for you, the reader, to provide further context and resources to support your successful implementation.

Mrs. Johnson and Brookdale Nations spent the year participating in proactive circles. This activity helped them gain a deeper sense of self-awareness and a new empathy for each other. They felt this was so impactful for them and their relationships within the school setting that they decided to create a plan to implement a conflict recovery system school-wide. They were careful to ensure cultural humility was the cornerstone and civility was insistent.

They collaborated and co-constructed the plan for the second half of the school year and planned to present their idea to the entire school, formally, at the end of the school year. After a lot of research on implementation models, they decided to go with The National Implementation Research Network's (NIRN) stages of implementation, which is a cross-disciplinary sequence of 6 stages. A summary of this can be found at https://safesupportivelearning.ed.gov/topic-research/program-implementation. *It is important to note that this is a long-term plan which will take years to implement fully. Patience is key.*

Before beginning, they decided they needed to state the goal of what they wanted to achieve and to decide on the community principles for the group.

They established team member roles (i.e., recorder, timekeeper, leader, presenter, etc.) and stated that the goal is full implementation of a restorative justice program at the school that involves the incorporation of cultural humility. Once those beginning steps were set, they started with their plan for implementation:

Phase 1- Exploration and Adoption:

The first stage is devoted to articulating the problem. Implementing conflict recovery and restoration was too vague a goal. This step will take months. The purpose is to funnel down to a goal supported by data. Conflict recovery has several layers, and different people interpret things differently. Brookdale Nations knows how important it is to have buy-in, so they decide they need to hear from those outside of the group. They decide to research and administer a needs assessment to Brookdale High students and staff to identify specific areas that need to be addressed.

Once this data was collected, they identified the needs and defined opportunities for change. They also planned to use this information to conduct interviews with stakeholders to ask the idealized question which is grounded in solution-focused principles, "If you woke up tomorrow and _____ change was apparent, what would that look like? How would that feel? etc." For example, Brookdale might see fewer office discipline referrals if restorative justice is the norm. This is directly connected to the ethos activity Dr. Dillinger walked professional learning community team through earlier.

Phase 2- Program Installation:

The second phase used the data and information from the first phase to develop objectives and outcomes. Included in and important to this step was to identify existing human, physical, or financial resources. NOTE: The NIRN suggests that these questions be asked:

- Do new policies need to be written to reflect the upcoming changes?
- Do existing staff members have the expertise to implement the identified solution, or are new hires necessary?
- Who will deliver the training, and when and where? How will staff and stakeholders be paid or compensated for attending the training?

- *How will the effectiveness of the training be measured, and how will ongoing learning be supported?*
- *Are our physical space, infrastructure, and equipment adequate?*
- *Can additional funding streams be sought to cover the long-term costs?*
- *What outcome measures will be watched, and how will progress be tracked? What are the benchmarks? What metrics will be used?*

Phase 3- Initial Implementation:

This stage focused on the actual implementation of the proposed changes. This stage takes note of the potential push-back from members in the school who for a variety of reasons might not be fully committed to the process. They expected there to be some push-back from students and personnel when they are asked to use new and different language, routines, documentation procedures, etc. This is why the members of Brookdale Nations strategically position themselves in conversations and model the behaviors and language regularly.

This stage should be devoted to supporting everyone at Brookdale High through those changes. It incorporated several practice proactive and recovery circles to let others weigh in on implementation and effectiveness. They even used the circles to address feedback and support Brookdale through the transition. They considered some of the suggested ideas from NIRN that included:

- *Professional development that is planned, intentional, and part of an ongoing, school-wide effort;*
- *School leaders serving as role models, cheerleaders, and facilitators;*
- *Ensure that teachers and other have the needed resources and partnerships for strong and effective implementation*
- *Organization and a structure that supports, encourages, and recognizes change efforts;*

Phase 4- Full Implementation:

Once everything with the implementation was normalized as the standard practice full implementation could be considered. Although, Brookdale was in the first stages, they anticipated this plan would be reflected system wide. They envisioned that Brookdale could be a shining example of how a school created a supportive and caring community where everyone is respected and valued, and their stories heard.

In this phase the team planned to assess if the needs have been met and what changes need to be added or adjusted. This would involve an annual evaluation of the program and the school's needs. The adopted NIRN suggestion to ask questions such as:

- *Are the outcome measures at the expected level of performance? Why or why not?*
- *Are the expected performance standards still appropriate?*
- *Have the goals of the community and district shifted since the program began? Is the program still aligned to the larger goals?*
- *What do Brookdale High personnel and students think of this program? Has it become expected practice and spread beyond Brookdale United?*

Phase 5- Innovation:

This phase will involve the development of a fidelity checklist or some other form of fidelity assessment. This is also the phase where adaptations are made that are unique to the needs of Brookdale High, and its population. They acknowledged that continued data collection and evaluation were essential to the implementation of Brookdale Nation thriving and not surviving.

Phase 6- Sustainability:

The final phase is not the last phase. The whole implementation process needs to long term cultivation, periodic revision, and consistent training of new members to Brookdale High.

FINAL THOUGHTS

In closing, the idea of implementing and practicing cultural humility and civility is multilayer, but, so too, are humans. It is necessary for mental health professionals to work in concert with administrators, teachers, students, and other personnel to advocate for the services that students need, but also for the strategies that will support a healthy school culture. Moreover, offer opportunities for students to co-construct how the school operates and how all values will be respected goes a long way to building trusting relationships. As a mental health professional, those health relationships are key to quality service. It is important to be authentic, genuine, and perhaps vulnerable. Most importantly, one must acknowledge and critically analyze the source of their personality and persona.

Take a moment to engage with the chapter's *think, reflect, connect* questions and the activity, *On the Table*. This was an activity presented in an earlier chapter. The next chapter discusses the implications for higher education institutions.

On the Table Activity

The authors provided an example activity, *On the Table*, designed to facilitate conversation about characteristics that are obvious or those that one might learn after a few conversations. Revisit that activity and take a moment to identify three unique attributes you have. Then, identify some stereotypes that are associated with those identities. For example, if you are a woman, identify some stereotypes associated with being a woman, and then identify how you are different from other women. Finally, think about how those identities and how your experiences have shaped you, influenced your personality, your interactions, and your understanding of others who are similar and dissimilar from you.

THINK, REFLECT, CONNECT

1. After reading *Brookdale United*'s implementation plan, what do you think is missing? What logistical challenges will the team face?
2. Which phase will be the hardest? Why? What are some things that can be done to avoid these challenges?
3. How do you see this plan working in your school? Who would be on the team? What changes need to be made to this plan? Take this time to begin thinking about how to initiate an action or strategic plan in your school. You can also find some free resources and templates for action planning at www.parkeredanddevelopment.com.

_____
_____
_____
_____
_____

REFERENCES

Hook, J. N., Davis, D., Owen, J., & DeBlaere, C. (2017). *Cultural humility: Engaging Diverse Identities in therapy.* Washington, DC: American Psychological Association.

Lambert, M. J., & Barley, D. E. (2001). Research summary on the therapeutic relationship and psychotherapy outcome. *Psychotherapy: Theory, Research, Practice, Training, 38*(4), 357–361. Doi: https://doi.org/10.1037/0033-3204.38.4.357

National Child Traumatic Stress Network, Justice Consortium, Schools Committee, and Culture Consortium. (2017). *Addressing race and trauma in the classroom: A resource for educators.* Los Angeles, CA, and Durham, NC: National Center for Child Traumatic Stress

Summary of NIRN's stages of implementation. (n.d.). Retrieved from https://safesupportivelearning.ed.gov/topic-research/program-implementation

Willard, M. (August 2018). A fresh start with restorative practices. Retrieved from https://www.schoolcounselor.org/newsletters/august-2018/a-fresh-start-with-restorative-practices?st=MT

Chapter 9

Considerations for Higher Education

> *"I find I am constantly being encouraged to pluck out some one aspect of myself and present this as the meaningful whole, eclipsing or denying the other parts of self."*
>
> —Audre Lorde

This book focused on K–12 primarily; however, the authors have generated additional considerations for higher education institutions. Many colleges and universities across the country have implemented various types of diversity programming. This type of programming usually amounts to diversity window dressings and is about optics and not always substance. The optics may not be a true reflection of the actual work colleges and universities are engaged in to create spaces where cultural humility can take root.

This chapter, while brief, will offer some of the considerations for colleges and universities to bring these concepts into focus so that the optics match the substance. And the substance is about action—action that addresses equity and inclusion, and considerations aimed at closing the diversity boutique of shining pretty things (programming) that celebrates and does not necessarily cultivate.

Let us first discuss a list of suggestions, and then the authors will present strategies that use the MOI framework for teaching value attributes along with academic content. These strategies can be particularly effective for educator programs of study and diversity offices across colleges and universities concerned with building programming that are effective, empowering, and empathetic.

The authors suggest higher education institutions focus on:

- Engaged training and programming that focuses on understanding and affirmation. Often times, diversity training focuses on what people should *not* do, say, or think. Cultural humility acknowledges diversity of thought, behaviors, actions, and thinking, and in the case of colleges and universities, these are premier place to explore those differences. This may allow people to come to consensus or collaboration, or it might help them negotiate conflict and compromise, as depicted on the Civility Control Scale.
- Proactive support and engagement from senior and executive administration is critical. As was discussed in chapter 4, it is a part of the leader's responsibility to set the tone, set the culture, and cultivate an ethos where cultural humility thrives. These leaders can also set in motion, conflict recovery, and restoration practices to support students and staff in navigating the intercultural crossover successfully.
- Use service-learning or other types of experiential programming to support the idea of cultural humility and civility. Engage students who are from differing backgrounds. This is important as colleges and universities enrolled more international students. This can be an excellent opportunity for students to engage in awareness, sensitivity, and responsiveness. The idea is that when students are working on experiential projects, it allows them to exercise and practice teaming, collaboration, empathy, humility, and a host of other attributes. These students may also be better positioned to advocate for the needs of others.
- Instructors and professors can incorporate exercises into their content to encourage greater understanding. This could include using activities like *What's on the Table* or *Who Do You Think I Am?* Instructors might also engage in strength-based assessments like the *Personality Package*™, developed by two of the authors of this book, to identify the characteristics of personality and persona that will help one develop the high-engagement relationships discussed in chapter 4. Personality bookends civility along with respect. When one source is their personality, what they uncover can affect their behavior, interactions, and can challenge or affirm long-held beliefs about others.

MODELING AND ASSESSING YOUR IMPACT

The MOI was introduced in the book, *Civility, Compassion, and Courage in Schools Today: Implementing Strategies for the K-12 classroom*. The authors developed the model, based on Krathwohl's affective hierarchy, created in 1964 (Kohler-Evans & Barnes, 2015). The model is a framework for developing and teaching social and emotional competencies to K–12 students and others. The overall goal is to promote embracing one's influence to engage in social change and to take action.

The MOI is presented in a hierarchical framework that moves one's thinking, behavior, and action from an awareness level to action (Kohler-Evans & Barnes, 2015). Much like the overarching concept of cultural humility, the framework however provides a step-by-step approach that school, college, and university official can use to focus on building the substantive action steps showcasing diversity initiative. The framework can be applied to support the understanding of social and emotional competencies and values in any educational context, and most importantly, to train teachers and other school professionals to engage in self-discovery, renewal, and recovery.

In the case of teacher education programs, the candidate has the opportunity to invest in learning about themselves and others. They might also benefit from engaging in deep conversations and dialogue with others from dissimilar backgrounds. The framework can guide one's perspective from cultural competency and proficiency to cultural humility. The next section takes each level of the MOI and describes how it can be used effectively to facilitate and encourage cultural humility.

LEVEL ONE: DEVELOPING AN AWARENESS OF CULTURAL HUMILITY

The first level of the MOI involves developing an awareness of the concept you are attempting to teach (Kohler-Evans & Barnes, 2015). This means that one must define, describe, and offering examples or models of cultural humility. As with any new concept or idea, one must take the time to build knowledge and then scaffold learning to ensure proper breadth and depth.

This allows for the learner to make connections and, perhaps, engage in rich conversations with others.

Additionally, at this level, both the facilitator and learner are engaged in teaching and learning from each other. While the defining of a term might seem simple, cultural humility is a term—a concept—that has layers and requires one to discuss the origin of the terms "culture and humble." Of course, this might be the case with any new term, or examining a new way thinking about a term. It may require a deeper study of the etymology and an explanation of why the term and the new meaning are important for understanding and further discussion.

LEVEL TWO: ACKNOWLEDGE BELIEFS AND VALUES OF SELF AND OTHERS

Each level of the MOI reflects a deepening of the knowledge and application of the information and builds on the previous level. The second level of the MOI suggests that all parties involved should engage in the acknowledgement of each other's values and beliefs (Kohler-Evans & Barnes, 2015). As it relates to cultural humility, this level requires a consideration of one's bias boundaries, stereotypes, generalizations, and affirmation of cultural identities.

In the college classroom, for example, people from similar and dissimilar backgrounds and histories convene in the same space. They may have team projects, engage in discussions that highlight their knowledge of others, or lack thereof. They might, with a good facilitator, have difficult conversations where they can openly discuss diverse thoughts in a brave space. As has been discussed throughout this book, the bias boundaries can influence their ability and willingness to step out of their comfort zone and create new spaces for thoughts and ideas to flourish. More importantly, this group is embarking upon one of the most significant goals of cultural humility, that is, discovery of self and uncovering the source of one's personality and persona.

LEVEL THREE: BENEFIT OF CULTURAL HUMILITY TO SELF AND OTHERS

The third level of the MOI requires a building upon the last two levels. In this third level all involved need to explore the benefit of engaging in cultural humility for self and others. For example, you might explore the benefit to self and others my addressing these initial questions:

- Why is it important to experience and give someone respect, grace, or recovery?
- What are the benefits of engaging in cultural humility for self and others?
- What will be gained by engaging in understanding self and others?
- How will it support and enhance the interactions, behaviors, and relationships between individuals?

This could be a difficult level to achieve, depending on how each previous level is facilitated. A significant realization of this level is recognizing that the benefit is multidimensional and can be quite visceral. It is a reckoning of one's personality with their values and beliefs, and the ways in which these new understandings shapes new behaviors and actions. It also acknowledges the need to make meaning of this new found knowledge or new experience to serve others in need and share a new scheme of thinking and understanding.

LEVEL FOUR: INFLUENCE AND ACTION

First, the concept of cultural humility is defined through the awareness level. Second, values, beliefs, and perspectives are affirmed and acknowledged. Third, there is a realization of the benefit to self and others. In this final step, all involved are empowered to take *action and embrace* his or her influence to become a *change enterprise*. A change enterprise is a person or group of people engaged in an intentional and purposeful action to shift thinking, behavior, and action toward a greater good. They are also encouraged to develop methods and ways to measure progress with fidelity.

The overall idea is once you understand what cultural humility is; you must do something with it. The knowledge gained only becomes useful when you take action. This might mean that multiple engagements will have to occur in order for the action to become sustainable. For example, it could result in sharing thoughts and ideas with various and different communities of learners. It might also be engaging in solution-focused approaches.

As it relates to both educator preparation programs and the overall college classroom, the students are essentially fostering strong bonds and high-engagement relationships. These relationships foster an insistence to make meaning of new learning and a desire to create change. These high-engagement relationships can be used to build bridges and foster compassionate, authentic, and meaningful interactions. The practice of cultural humility fades the other-izing and support showing genuine care for others and an exploration of self to better understand others.

FINAL THOUGHTS

In closing, cultural humility is an infinite recycling of awareness, sensitivity, and responsiveness to new experiences and thinking—experiences and thinking that might disrupt or affirm one's current understanding. Through cultural humility, bias boundaries collapse and false narratives fail to speak to one's individuality. As one opens his or her mind and lives to learning about others, the destructiveness that often creates systems of oppression, the actions and behaviors that illustrate discrimination, and the thinking and attitudes that feed micro- and macro-aggressions, are shattered. From those shattered pieces of division and cultural blindness, rich opportunities to demonstrate authentic inclusionary and equity practices emerge—practices that can affirm and respect all cultural identities. The college and university classrooms can be fertile ground to ensure this happens.

THINK, REFLECT, CONNECT

1) How can K–12 schools and higher education institutions work in unison to ensure cultural humility, in particular, and civility are realized?
2) How might you use the MOI in your educational setting to build solid and substantive programming that reflect action and not just the celebratory activities like Black History Month, Women's History Month, LGBTQ+ awareness events, and so on?
3) Based on your experiences, what might be the most difficult level and how would you get started? Your first step, and what would be your desired outcome?

REFERENCE

Kohler-Evans, P. & Barnes, C. D. (2015). *Civility, compassion, and courage in school today: Strategies for implementing in K-12 classrooms*. Landam, MD: Rowman-Littlefield Publisher.

Chapter 10

Bringing It All Together

"Diversity may be the hardest thing for a society to live with, and perhaps the most dangerous thing for a society to be without."

—*William Sloane Coffin*

Conflict recovery is a multilayered concept that when operationalized can provide a system—a process designed to renew, repair, and rebuild relationships. The essence of conflict recovery is a return to a desired state of being. What the authors have proposed in this book is the idea that when one is compelled to find this desired state of being, it should be fostered through cultural humility and civility.

Throughout this book, the intersection of cultural humility and civility was the driving force. Frameworks were presented to display how the concepts aligned and various other considerations were provided to increase one's awareness of how and why the topic should be incorporated into educational/school settings. Brookdale High was used to example ways to implement and incorporate conflict recovery and use cultural humility to strengthen interactions and the development of high-engagement relationships.

In chapter 1, the authors made a case for why this topic is important and valuable in the K–12 educational settings. Schools across the country are faced with daily academic demands. Students and staff are under extreme pressure to succeed and show academic excellence. However, what schools must pay attention to is how the culture and climate creates a space for deep learning and growing to occur—learning that can be both academic and social and emotional. This type of learning happens best in relationship-driven environments where trust and care are evident.

Chapter 2 provided an in-depth review of the origins of cultural humility and the elements of cultural humility—awareness, sensitivity, and responsiveness—were discussed. The chapter also presented information on the civility crisis and the decline of civility across the nation. Cultural humility originated in the social sciences to encourage individuals to engage in an understanding of self and others.

This single idea denotes the capital reason why one needs to shift away from the ending point of competence to cultural humility. Educators must engage in understanding themselves. They must then acknowledge their contributions and be willing to criticize a system that fails many of their students. When educators can engage in that level of awareness, it allows them to be sensitive to the students' needs and respond to those needs in a positive way. It is also important that students are encouraged to do the same, in terms of exercising cultural humility and civility toward the adults in the building.

Chapters 3, 4, and 5 led the reader into a deeper understanding of cultural humility, how cultural humility should be embraced in education, and the paradigm shift from competency and proficiency to humility. The cultural humility and civility framework was presented to show how one's thinking, behavior, and actions are aligned to each elements of cultural humility. The framework also highlighted respect and personality as key to ensuring authenticity and believability of self to others. This chapter was the final chapter in the section to set the stage for the introduction of Brookdale High, a school that reflects the demographic changes and cultural diaspora in schools across the country.

The next section of the book focused on teaching, leading, and counseling. Each chapter highlighted the people, policies, and practices that can make cultural humility and civility a normalized way of being. Each chapter also integrated the idea of conflict recovery and how the concept can be used effectively to move the culture and ethos. Chapter 6 introduced

Brookdale High, and capitalized on using cultural humility and civility to develop high-engagement relationships and also described conflict recovery in detail.

The leading chapter, chapter 7, focused on the sights and sounds, the freedom and flexibility, and the soul and spirit of a school that drives the school's culture. This chapter also presented to concept of ethos—the cultural spirit of the school and how ethos and culture are intertwined. It cannot be said enough that the leader sets the tone in a school and is the chief instructional officer, disciplinarian, and motivator.

Therefore, the leader has to keep an eye on internal and external factors that will interrupt or disrupt a healthy culture for learning. This chapter provided activities, as did the previous chapters, to address how one might engage teams in thinking about the culture, and how collectively one might achieve the desired culture where success and growth is measured individually and in groups.

Chapter 8 focused on cultural humility and civility from a mental health professional's perspective. The chapter began with a justification for the shift from a competence mindset to a cultural humility mindset, specifically from a school-based mental health standpoint. The chapter then entered into a discussion of restorative justice principles and presented ideas to initiate an effective implementation process using Brookdale High as an example to outline a strategic action plan.

Other ideas were presented, such as peer circles that can be a part of a larger conflict recovery process. What is clear is that conflict recovery built on cultural humility and civility can increase one's cultural intelligence and allow one to build a dynamic opportunity to engage in deep equity and inclusion. As schools evolve and change, cultural intelligent educators will be a key factor to the success of these schools.

Finally, chapter 9 presented a discussion of cultural humility in the college and university classroom, with a specific focus on educator preparation programs. The chapter used the MOI to present a systematic way of facilitate and implement cultural humility, specifically in the college classroom to empower students to embrace their ability to take action and become effective social agents of change—a change enterprise and increase their cultural intelligence.

Chapter 10

THE POWER OF CULTURAL INTELLIGENCE

There are different types of intelligence; however, one that seems to be lacking in society in general is cultural intelligence. Cultural intelligence—intercultural understanding and interactions that allow someone to acknowledge:

- Group behaviors.
- Individual behavior, values, and beliefs.
- Universal behaviors that are not based on an individual or groups but exist across groups.

Arguably, this type of intelligence has yet to be normed in our society. In part, culture is directly aligned to race, and ethnicity, and those topics are visceral and uncomfortable to discuss for some individuals. However, until those topics can be a normal part of the conversation, cultural intelligence will continue to elude those with perceived power and those from marginalized groups.

We live in a world where intercultural crossover is inevitable. People are transient and communities are diversifying. In the past, humans could spend their entire lives surrounded by peers that were like them; however, in today's world with social media as the greatest information transporter, cultures that are dissimilar from one's own is everywhere. It is becoming increasingly difficult to stay within the narrow box of sameness. When people are engaged in learning about the richness and beauty in other cultures, it only stands to enrich their own lives.

Couple that with the changing demographics in this country, intercultural understanding will become even more important. Individuals will need to learn how to understand, engage, and interact with people who are different—people who may have unfamiliar backgrounds, histories, value systems, and experiences. It will allow one to enter into new worlds. Engaging in such a way will make it impossible to interact with those who think like you, look like you, and who have the same belief system as you. This is critically meaningful as students leave their K–12 experiences to enter college or begin their careers.

RECOMMENDATIONS, NEXT STEPS, AND FINAL THOUGHTS

Ultimately, the questions are these:

1) What is one small change that you can make today to work toward a civility and a cultural humility mindset?
2) What are the next steps for your team and your school?

As you think about your next steps, the following are some recommendations to ponder:

- Start small. This might mean forming a small group of interested people to engage in a book talk or discussion about cultural humility. This may help create buy-in from the overall staff.
- Change the language and address anything in the ethos—the culture, that might hinder progress to the implementation of cultural humility of civility principles.
- Seek expert training from professionals who are well versed in equity and inclusion and restorative justice. They can help you implement a sustainable plan. The last thing you want is for the process to be forfeited before you get it off the ground because of inexperience and dissension.
- Conduct a needs assessment to determine where and how the culture is being challenged. You will need to be strategic in how you collect this data. Most people will indicate a culture is fine and there is no intercultural tension in an attempt to avoid engaging in uncomfortable conversations. Humans are prone to categorize and therefore we are not prone to admit our biases.
- Engage in a cultural humility self-assessment. Self-awareness takes practice and training. This requires intrapersonal and interpersonal development. It may challenge your professional standards and practices. It might also motivate you to realign your thinking, action, and behavior toward others. Finally, this type of assessment may mean that you question the culture within your school, community, and other groups.

In closing, diversity, equity, and inclusion are front and center in our national and global conversations and policy discussions. The demographic trends are pushing this country closer and closer to an intercultural crossover. This is clearly seen in K–12 education, especially in public schools where you have a majority of staff who are white and students from various minority groups.

These staff members falsely believe themselves to be culturally competent when the desired outcomes should be cultural humility that leads to civility. It will be increasingly important that adults and the students engage in opportunities to increase their awareness of each other stories and backgrounds. It will be just as important that each of these groups engage in self-reflection and discovery. This will only serve to foster successful interactions and engagements. These meaningful engagements will speak to the personal stories and authentic narratives that one shares. The person is the expert and narrator of his or her own story. The narrative will not be based upon what someone else believes his or her story should be.

Humility is again the freedom from arrogance, assumptions, and acidic commentary designed to harm others. How different would your school be if you could engage this idea on a daily basis? How would your culture look, feel, and sound if you could build upon the idea of cultural humility to deploy conflict recovery when the relationship needs repairing? How engaging would the learning environment be if the members were acutely aware of who they are and how those backgrounds, histories, and narratives add to the richness—the soul and spirit of the school?

Cultural humility is a meaningful and intentional endeavor to respond to the needs and strengths of the students and staff. It is a valuable process designed to serve humanity with dignity and respect. It should be the heartbeat of school. Those who believe that every student has the right to find and walk their pathway toward success should be champion cultural humility and civility and stand in the gap, to help close the gap of intercultural tension in schools.

About the Authors

Candice Dowd Barnes, EdD, is an associate professor at the University of Central Arkansas in the Department of Elementary, Literacy, and Special Education. She is also the chief operations officer for Parker Education & Development, LLC. She strongly believes in the power of authentic learning experiences and relationships to teach beyond the walls of the classroom into all aspects of life.

Dr. Barnes has an extensive background in early childhood education, equity and inclusion, and educational leadership. She is a dynamic speaker and accomplished author of multiple publications on relationships, coaching, cultural humility and civility, group dynamics, and equity and inclusion. Dr. Barnes has presented nationally and internationally on conflict recovery, the intersection of cultural humility and civility, humility, equity, and inclusion, and personality coaching.

She is the coauthor of *Civility, Compassion and Courage in Schools Today: Strategies for Implementing in K-12 Classrooms* and *Success Favors Well-prepared Adults: Developing Routines and Relationships to Improve School Culture*. She is also the codeveloper of the *Culture, Humility, and Civility Training Program*, certified by the International Civility Trainers' Consortium. In her spare time, she makes craft jewelry under the name PersonalityCrafting.

Chayla Rutledge Slaton, ABD, is a school psychology PhD candidate at the University of Central Arkansas and a research assistant in the Department of Elementary, Literacy, and Special Education. She believes that every man, woman, and child has strengths that make them unique and define who they are.

Chayla has a background in psychology, specifically school psychology. She has coauthored multiple publications on relationships, teaching strategies, and cultural humility. Her dissertation is dedicated to student's perceptions of their teacher's cultural humility and how belongingness moderates the relationship between student's perceptions of their teacher's cultural humility and their working alliance with their teacher.

As an executive coach and CEO of Parker Education & Development, LLC, **Todd Scott Parker** distinguishes himself through his ability to deliver coaching and training in a dynamic way to various educational and business audiences. His work is both unique and creative. He blends evidenced-based strategies, techniques, and methods from education and business to help schools, small businesses, and other organizations to create sustainable models of success.

Todd is a dynamic keynote speaker and poet. He is the coauthor of *Success Favors Well-Prepared Teachers: Developing Relationships and Routines to Improve School Culture*. He created Kuu-Bro, an initiative for young men and boys to find their natural leadership abilities. He developed a peer-to-peer mentoring program—A Better Citizen (ABC)—which has received local and national attention, and he developed the Personality Package™—a strength-based assessment process to source the behaviors that will enhance interactions and engagement with others. He is also the codeveloper of the *Culture, Humility, and Civility Training Program*, certified by the International Civility Trainers' Consortium.

www.ingramcontent.com/pod-product-compliance
Lightning Source LLC
Chambersburg PA
CBHW060342170426
43202CB00014B/2856